THIS BOOK
BELONGS TO:

LANCELOT

The Adventures of King Arthur's Most Celebrated Knight

CHILDREN'S CLASSICS

This unique series of Children's Classics™ features accessible and highly readable texts paired with the work of talented and brilliant illustrators of bygone days to create fine editions for today's parents and children to rediscover and treasure. Besides being a handsome addition to any home library, this series features faux leather spines stamped in gold, full-color illustrations, and high-quality acid-free paper that will enable these books to be passed from one generation to the next.

Adventures of Huckleberry Finn
The Adventures of Tom Sawyer
Aesop's Fables
Alice's Adventures in Wonderland
Andersen's Fairy Tales
Anne of Avonlea
Anne of Green Gables
At the Back of the North Wind
Black Beauty
The Call of the Wild
A Child's Book of Country Stories
A Child's Book of Stories
A Child's Book of Stories from Many Lands
A Child's Christmas
A Child's Garden of Verses
A Christmas Carol and Other Christmas Stories
Cinderella and Other Classic Italian Fairy Tales
The Complete Mother Goose
Goldilocks and the Three Bears and Other Classic English Fairy Tales
Great Dog Stories
Grimm's Fairy Tales
Hans Brinker *or* The Silver Skates
Heidi
The Hound of the Baskervilles
Joan of Arc
The Jungle Book
Just So Stories
Kidnapped
King Arthur and His Knights
Lancelot: The Adventures of King Arthur's Most Celebrated Knight
The Legend of Pocahontas
A Little Child's Book of Stories
Little Men
A Little Princess
Little Women
Peter Pan
Pollyanna
The Prince and the Pauper
Rebecca of Sunnybrook Farm
Robin Hood
Robinson Crusoe
The Secret Garden
The Sleeping Beauty and Other Classic French Fairy Tales
The Swiss Family Robinson
Tales from Shakespeare
Tales of Pirates and Buccaneers
Through the Looking Glass and What Alice Found There
Treasure Island
A Very Little Child's Book of Stories
The Wind in the Willows
The Wonderful Wizard of Oz

THE ADVENTURES OF KING ARTHUR'S MOST CELEBRATED KNIGHT

Formerly published as *Arthur and His Knights*

By Christine Chaundler

Illustrated by Thomas MacKenzie and Eleanor Fortescue Brickdale

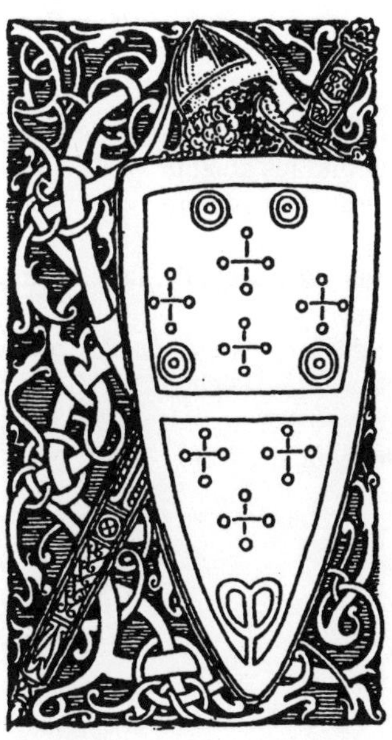

CHILDREN'S CLASSICS
New York • Avenel

Portions of this book were originally published in *Arthur and His Knights.*

This edition is published by Children's Classics, an imprint and trademark of
Random House Value Publishing, Inc.,
40 Engelhard Avenue, Avenel, New Jersey 07001.

Printed and bound in the United States of America

Library of Congress Cataloging-in-Publication Data

Chaundler, Christine.
Lancelot : the adventures of King Arthur's most celebrated knight / Christine Chaundler;
Formerly published in Arthur and his knights
[Illustrated by Eleanor Fortescue Brickdale].
p. cm.
Summary: A collection of tales featuring the bravest knight in King Arthur's court.
ISBN 0-517-14636-3
1. Lancelot (Legendary character)—Legends. 2. Arthurian romances—Adaptations.
[1. Lancelot (Legendary character)—Legends. 2. Knights and knighthood—Folklore.
3. Folklore—England.]
I. Brickdale, Eleanor Fortescue, ill. II. Title.
PZ8.1.C395Lan 1995
[398.22]—dc20 95-10994
CIP
AC

Cover design by Bill Akunevicz, Jr.
Production supervision by Roméo Enriquez
Editorial supervision by Claire Booss and Nina Rosenstein

10 9 8 7 6 5 4 3 2 1

CONTENTS

CONTENTS

LIST OF COLOR ILLUSTRATIONS

Opposite Page

PREFACE TO THIS ILLUSTRATED EDITION

The shimmering surfaces of the beautiful paintings in this volume welcome us into the magical kingdom of Arthur's legendary knights.

The major portion of the illustrations were created by Thomas MacKenzie, a British painter, etcher, and wood engraver. His brilliant work in children's book illustration is considered by many to be the finest of its period—the early twentieth century.

There are only two paintings by Eleanor Fortescue Brickdale, but they are so exquisite that their presence seems greater: her portrait of Lancelot on the cover and the touching scene of his embrace with Guinevere. Eleanor Fortescue Brickdale was an illustrator, painter, and designer who also worked in England early in the twentieth century.

These scenes, together with the ones by Thomas MacKenzie, illuminate the spell that the legend of Lancelot has woven throughout five centuries.

Claire Booss
Series Editor

1995

FOREWORD

In the days of chivalry, during the glorious reign of the legendary King Arthur, lived Sir Lancelot, the noblest knight in all of history. This is the story of the daring exploits that sent his name soaring across the globe—and of the darker side of his life and the sorrows he suffered. But let's start at the beginning. In those days long, long ago, justice was decided by the sword, and danger lurked everywhere. Into this chaos came the wise and powerful wizard Merlin, who helped establish a small boy as the true heir to the throne of England. With Merlin's counsel, the boy Arthur grew up to be the greatest king of all time. King Arthur created the fellowship of Knights of the Round Table, whose mission was the mastery of goodness over evil. Sir Lancelot was King Arthur's favorite knight.

The story of King Arthur and his knights has been passed down from generation to generation for hundreds of years. Were King Arthur and Lancelot real people in history? These men probably did exist many years ago, but historians can only trace their names through the threads of literature. Unlike facts, legends are inherited and then refashioned over time. Legend has shaped the story of a mighty warrior named Arthur, who was first mentioned—only briefly—in a Welsh poem in the year 600. Over the next few centuries, writers further described "Arthur" as a Celtic warrior who vanquished Saxon invaders. In the twelfth century, Arthur's legend gained richness and color as Geoffrey of Monmouth, in his *History of the Kings of Britain,* named Arthur the conqueror of Western Europe and painted many more details of his life and his reign. In the thirteenth century, the story was infused with a religious theme of Christianity.

Lancelot's name, too, was plucked out of ancient history—from the Irish myths of the sun god Lug—and Lancelot joined the Arthurian folklore, journeying through the centuries in a variety of Welsh, British, and French writings. The age of chivalry captured the imagination of writers and poets throughout the world. Today, the venerable Lancelot and King Arthur have taken their mythological place in history, regaled in story and song, among the most beloved heroes of all time.

In this delightful retelling of the legend of Lancelot and his adventures in Camelot—the court of King Arthur—author Christine Chaundler takes us back to an age of faith, with gallant knights and their deeds of valor, a time of heroic loves, spiritual quests, and, simply, the enchantment of Camelot. Chaundler's crisp and compelling narrative begins with the early days of the wizard Merlin, chronicles the rise to power of young King Arthur—including the miracle of the sword in the stone, Arthur's encounter with the Lady of the Lake, and his marriage to Queen Guinevere—then follows Sir Lancelot through his many dangerous escapades as champion of the downtrodden and savior of damsels in distress. This unforgettable epic comes to a close as the idealized society of Camelot fades into history.

Christine Chaundler, a children's editor in England and the author of dozens of books, was most popular for her stories of schoolgirls in the 1920s and 1930s. "As the eldest member of a large Victorian family—eldest to survive infancy that is—I have always had much to do with children. Most of my work has been for them. I am also greatly interested in folklore and in psychic things," she once said. Chaundler's love of folklore breathes new life into this vivid celebration of the golden age of chivalry.

The Knights of the Round Table were sworn to help the oppressed, always ready to meet bold challenges with honesty, loyalty, kindness, and courage, and to prove their mettle in jousting tournaments. But knights had human temptations and flaws, too. Burning in the heart of Sir Lancelot, faithful and beloved follower of King Arthur, was an undying and hopeless love for his queen, Guinevere. For

Guinevere, Lancelot forswore all other women; for Guinevere, Lancelot vanquished all enemies; and for Guinevere, Lancelot descended, for a time, into madness. In this book you will also meet other knights, both faithful and fearsome, and follow them through dark mysteries and healing magic, through knightly pursuits and tragedies of love. Chaundler recounts the star-crossed love story of Tristram and Isolde and tells the tale of the purest knight of all, Sir Galahad, and his spiritual quest of the Holy Grail.

In *Lancelot: The Adventures of King Arthur's Most Celebrated Knight,* Christine Chaundler takes us on an exhilarating tour of the life of the exalted Sir Lancelot. We meet the fair Elaine, who suffers a hopeless and unrequited love for Lancelot, and we accompany Lancelot as he saves his queen, cures the sick, and rides evermore in search of adventures. With all the energy and excitement of the days of roughshod knights and gentle ladies, of courtliness and destiny fulfilled, we experience in *Lancelot* the wonder and magic of one of the greatest epics of all time.

NINA ROSENSTEIN

Westfield, New Jersey
1995

LANCELOT

The Adventures of King Arthur's Most Celebrated Knight

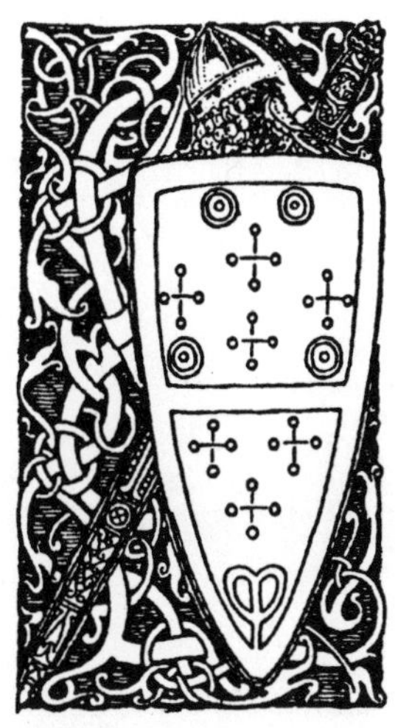

THE GREAT MAGICIAN

LONG, long ago, so long ago that it was almost in fairy-tale times, there lived in England a great magician named Merlin. He was very wise and very powerful, and he did many wonderful deeds of magic, so that everybody looked upon him with awe and reverence and paid great attention to everything that he said. Nobody quite knew who he was or where he had come from, though there were many mysterious legends told about his birth. But this is the story of how he first became known in England.

There was at the time a king named Vortigern. He ought not really to have been king at all, for there were two princes named Aurelius and Uther who had more right to the throne of England than he. But when their father had died these two princes had been only children, and Vortigern had usurped the crown from them and made himself king. But his wicked deed did not bring him any happiness. All through his reign he was constantly fighting against his enemies, and towards the end of his life heathen tribes descended upon the land and overran it, and Vortigern was obliged to fly with the remainder of his army into the mountains of Wales.

Even amongst the mountains the king did not feel safe, and he made up his mind that he would build himself a strong tower upon the highest mountain, so that he might shut himself up in it and end his life in peace.

Snowdon was the highest of the mountains, and here the king determined to build his tower. He collected great quantities of stones and mortar, and sent for many workmen to build the castle. But though the men toiled hard and raised many stones one upon another they did not make much progress. For each night, when darkness fell, all that they had built during the day fell down. For many weeks they laboured, but it was no use. They could not build the castle, and at last they had to go to the king and tell him that the work could not be done.

Vortigern was very disturbed when he heard this. He sent for all the wizards and wise men that he knew, and asked them to tell him how he might build his castle. The wizards consulted long and earnestly together, and at last they told the king that if he could find a man who was born of no earthly father, and should mix his blood with the mortar that the masons used, then the castle walls would be made sure and would not fall down.

Vortigern immediately sent messengers through all the country to try and discover such a man. For a long while the messengers met with no success in their search; but at last they came to a town where they found a young man whose father was known of none. So they seized him and carried him away to the king. And this young man was Merlin.

The king was overjoyed when Merlin was brought before him, for he thought that he had found the man whose blood would make his castle sure. But Merlin laughed scornfully when he heard for what purpose his blood was required.

'My blood will not bind your tower together, my lord king,' he cried. 'Bring these prophets before me who have prophesied these things. Liars are they—and liars I will prove them to be.'

The king sent for the wise men, and when they were come Merlin asked them a question.

'Masters,' said he, 'I pray you tell me the reason why the king's castle falleth?'

But this was just what the wizards did not know. They looked at one another in troubled silence and made no reply to Merlin's question.

Then Merlin said :

'If you cannot tell why the castle falleth, how can you know for certain that my blood will cause it to endure ? Make plain to us now what troubleth the foundations, then may we the better understand how your remedy will bind the walls fast.'

Still the wizards did not speak, and Merlin turned to the king.

'Sire, listen to me,' he said. 'Beneath the foundations of your castle there lies a deep pool of water. It is owing to what is hidden in this pool that your building falleth to the ground each night. Bid your men dig, and you will see that I speak truly.'

The king, anxious to see how much this strange young man knew, told his men to dig as Merlin directed. And when the men had dug deep enough they found that sure enough, beneath the spot on which they had been trying to build the castle, there was a pool of water. Then Merlin stepped forward and cried :

'Masters and great magicians, tell us now what lies hidden beneath the dark waters of this pool.'

But the wizards dared not say a word, for they had no idea of what might lie hidden in the waters, and they were growing dreadfully afraid of this young man, who, for all his youth, knew so much more than they.

Then Merlin turned again to the king.

'Order your servants to dig trenches to draw off the water from this pool,' he said. 'Then you shall see that at the bottom there lie two dragons, one white, the other crimson as blood. It is these monsters that have troubled the earth at night and so caused your building to fall down.'

And when the water had been drawn off from the pool, there at the bottom lay the two dragons, just as Merlin had said.

Then Vortigern saw that Merlin was a far greater magician than any of the wise men in whose advice he had hitherto trusted. He asked the youth many questions about the future and what would happen to him. But Merlin had nothing good to tell him.

'Much evil have you done to your land,' he said. 'And now much evil shall come to you. You are as a man against whom the arrows are loosened on both sides. On the one side come the heathen to do you a mischief; on the other come the rightful heirs of the kingdom, Aurelius and Uther, to pluck the crown from your head. You shall perish and Aurelius shall be king for a short time. Then shall his brother Uther Pendragon reign, and after Uther shall come a king who shall be greater than any that has reigned in England before, or shall reign in England again.'

Vortigern listened in fear and trembling to Merlin's words. He would have liked to have kept this wonderful man always with him, but Merlin would have nothing to do with such a wicked king. When he had finished speaking he went out from the king's presence, and Vortigern never saw him again.

After he had gone, Vortigern fled to another castle and furnished it with food and stores. He did not stay to finish his tower on Snowdon, for he knew from Merlin's words that he would not have time. He fortified the castle as strongly as he could, hoping to escape the doom Merlin had prophesied for him, but it was all in vain. The two brothers, Aurelius and Uther, marched against him with a mighty army and burned his castle to the ground, and the king perished in the flames.

Then Aurelius turned upon the heathen tribes who were laying England waste, and after many great battles he succeeded in subduing them. The great lords and barons wanted to make Aurelius king, but before he would allow himself to be crowned Aurelius said that he wished to make a great monument in memory of all the brave men who had been killed by the heathen.

'First,' he said, 'I will that all the churches and monasteries that have been destroyed by the enemy shall be rebuilt, and when that is done I will not rest until I have raised a memorial for these men that shall last unto the world's end.'

So, first of all, the churches and monasteries and abbeys were rebuilt, and then, acting on the advice of his nobles, Aurelius sent for Merlin, to ask him to help him in his great undertaking. Merlin came willingly to serve under such a good king, and when he heard how Aurelius wished to build a monument that would endure for ever, he told him that in Ireland there were some wonderful stones of which such a monument might well be made.

'Once,' he said, 'there was a giant in Ireland who laboured greatly to build a circle of stones. He carried these stones himself from Africa, and they are so huge and weighty that a man now may not stir the least of them though he put forth all his strength.'

'Then how shall we bring them to this country, since they are so heavy?' asked Aurelius. 'And why should we send to Ireland for stones? Have we not in this realm stones enough and to spare?'

'Nay, king,' said Merlin. 'We have no such stones as these. For they are possessed of great merit, so that if sick men be bathed in the water with which they have been washed, they may be made whole from whatever hurt was upon them. There are no stones in the world which will make such an enduring monument as the stones the giant brought to Ireland long ago.'

Then all the nobles and barons were eager that the king should send for these wonderful stones. So ships were made ready for the expedition, and Uther, the king's brother, was made captain, and Merlin went with them to give his advice, and the fleet set sail for Ireland to bring the magic stones across the sea.

When the ships reached Ireland, however, and the Irish people heard for what reason the Britons had come to their country, they pelted them with stones and said that those should be the only stones the intruders should carry away. But when the Britons landed and advanced upon them, the Irish people fled, and left Uther and his knights to accomplish in peace the errand upon which they came.

Then Merlin led the knights to the mountain of Kildare, upon the summit of which lay the magic stones. The Britons had never seen such enormous stones before, and they stared at them doubtfully, wondering how they should carry them across the sea. But Merlin cast a spell upon the huge blocks, so that for all their great size they became as light as pebbles. Then the knights were able to lift them easily and, carrying them to the ships, they set sail for England again.

When they reached their own shores, they carried the stones to a place where there had once been a great massacre of Britons by the invading tribes. And when once they had been set in position, the enchantment made by Merlin departed from the stones and they became heavy again, so that no man was able to move even the smallest of them from the place where they were set. Then all the people flocked to see the magic stones, and Aurelius came from London, and a great feast was held upon the spot. And when Aurelius had dedicated the stones to the memory of the men who had fallen, he allowed his nobles to crown him king.

THE GREAT MAGICIAN

All this happened a long time ago, so long ago that nobody quite knows now how much of it is true and how much of it is just a story from fairy-tale times. But in the south of England, on Salisbury Plain, there is a circle of enormous stones which is called to-day Stonehenge. And people say that these are the magic stones which Merlin brought from Ireland, so that Aurelius might build a monument which would last to the world's end.

HOW ARTHUR CAME TO HIS KINGDOM

As Merlin had prophesied, the good king Aurelius did not reign very long. Very soon after he had been crowned, he fell sick and after many months of suffering he died.

Uther, his brother, was away in Wales at the time, fighting against a son of the wicked king Vortigern, who was trying to make trouble for Aurelius. One night a marvellous star appeared in the sky. It was a comet, and had a long beam of light, at the end of which there seemed to be a dragon's head. Uther was very disturbed at the sight of this star, and he called for Merlin, who was with him, and asked him what it might mean.

When Merlin saw the comet, he was so overcome with grief that he could not at first answer Uther. Then he told him that the star betokened that his brother Aurelius was dead, and that the appearance of the dragon in the sky meant that Uther himself was now the King of England.

HOW ARTHUR CAME TO HIS KINGDOM

Uther was very grieved to hear of the death of his brother. He made haste to finish his fighting and hurried back to England, where he found that all that Merlin had told him was true. Aurelius was dead, and he himself now reigned in his place.

Uther was a very brave man and he won many battles for his people. He caused a golden image to be made of a dragon, in memory of the dragon that had appeared in the sky, and always when he went to fight he had it borne before him into battle. Because of this he was called Uther Pendragon by his people, who loved him because of his bravery and his hardihood in fight.

But although he was a brave man, he was not always a very good one. And he did one very dishonourable thing which brought much trouble upon him. He fell in love with the wife of one of his earls, and he made war upon the earl and killed him in order that he might marry her, although the earl had always been faithful and loyal to him. And it was this which brought him trouble, for when his first baby was born, a little boy named Arthur, he was obliged to send him away from his court in order that he might be brought up secretly. For he was afraid lest some of the friends of the dead earl might kill the little fellow in order to be revenged upon the king for the good man's death.

It was to Merlin that Uther gave his little son, and Merlin carried the baby to a brave and honest knight named Ector and asked him to bring the child up as his own. Sir Ector already had one small son of his own, but he felt sorry for the little fellow, who, he thought, possessed no father or mother, and he took him and brought him up as his own child, never dreaming that it was the son of the king upon whom he had taken pity. He and his wife did not tell Arthur that he was only an adopted child, and Arthur grew up with his foster-brother, Kay, and the two boys were very happy together, and never guessed that they were not really brothers.

At last King Uther fell ill and died, and then there was great quarrelling amongst his lords as to who should be king after him. None of them knew that Uther had a son; and Merlin, the wise man, who alone of all in the kingdom knew the truth of Arthur's birth, said nothing then. For he knew that a child of Arthur's age would be helpless in the hands of these nobles, and he waited until he should be older before he brought him forth to the people as their king.

HOW ARTHUR CAME TO HIS KINGDOM

Then there came a sad time for England. The nobles were so busy fighting amongst themselves as to which of them should be king, that they had no time to fight against the savage tribes that were constantly invading the country and laying it waste. For very many years England was without a proper ruler, and there was great trouble and distress throughout the land.

At last, however, the time came when Arthur was old enough to be made king. Merlin, who had been watching over the boy secretly all these years, knew that the moment had arrived. But the great magician knew that it would be no use to bring the boy before the nobles and say: 'This is Uther's son.' For he knew that they would not believe him. So instead he went to the Archbishop of Canterbury and told him to call all the lords and knights of the realm to London to keep the feast of Christmas.

'For God will show us then by a miracle who shall be king,' he said.

So the Archbishop sent for all the great nobles and asked them to come to London to keep the feast of Christmas. And very early in the morning on Christmas Day, before it was light, the great Cathedral was filled with men, praying to God to send them a sign to show who was the rightful king of England.

And while they were praying, the miracle that Merlin had prophesied took place. When the service was over and the nobles came out into the courtyard of the Cathedral, they saw in the middle of it a great square stone of marble. On the marble stone there was an anvil of steel, and in the anvil there was a sword fixed, and on the sword there were golden letters which said :

'Whoso pulleth this sword out of this stone is rightwise born king of all England.'

The nobles flocked about the stone wondering at the words which were written on the sword, and some of them went back to tell the Archbishop, who hurried out to see the miracle. When the good man had seen the stone and read the mystic words, he commanded the nobles to go back into the Cathedral and pray to God once more.

'Let no man touch the sword until he hath taken counsel in prayer,' he said. And he went back into the Cathedral and celebrated mass again.

Then, after he had prayed earnestly to God to show whom He had chosen to be king, the Archbishop led the nobles out into the courtyard; and, one by one, each man tried to pull the sword out of the anvil. But none of them were able even to move it as it lay in the stone.

'He who shall be king of England is not here,' said the Archbishop. 'But doubt not—God will make him known in His own good time.'

Then the nobles chose ten knights from amongst themselves to keep watch over the stone until the man should be found who might draw the magic sword. And they arranged to hold a great tournament on New Year's Day. And they sent word that all the knights in the land should come to it and joust with one another upon horseback and show their skill at arms, hoping that they might in this way discover a man strong enough to draw the sword from the anvil.

Kay, the young son of Sir Ector, had been made knight a short while before, and he and his father came to London to joust at the tournament. With them came Arthur. He was not yet old enough to be made a knight himself, but he was proud and glad to think that his brother was able to take part in the tournament, and he was longing to see him distinguish himself in the lists.

But just before the little party reached the field where the tournament was to be held, Kay discovered that he had forgotten his sword. He had left it at the lodging where they had passed the night, and turning to his younger brother, he begged him to ride back and fetch it for him. Arthur at once turned his horse and rode back to the lodging. But when he reached it, he found that he could not enter. All the people who lived there had gone to watch the great tournament, and the doors were locked and barred.

Then Arthur was very angry.

'My brother shall not be without a sword this day!' he said to himself. And he remembered the sword stuck in the anvil in the courtyard of the Cathedral. He was only a boy, and though no doubt he had heard the story of the miracle, he did not understand its full meaning, or realise that only he who should be king of England might hope to draw the sword. It seemed to be the only chance of getting a weapon for his brother, and full of determination he mounted his horse again and rode off in haste to the Cathedral.

There was nobody in the courtyard when he reached it, for the knights who usually guarded the sword had all gone to the jousting, so Arthur found nobody to stop him as he made his way to where the great stone lay. He grasped the sword by the hilt and pulled it boldly—and the sword came out of the anvil as easily as though he had been drawing it from its scabbard. Then, full of eager delight at having found such a splendid sword for his brother, Arthur leapt on his horse's back again and galloped to the field where the tournament was to be held.

When Kay saw the sword, he recognised it as the sword of the stone, and, very perplexed and troubled, he went to his father and told him what had happened. Sir Ector, too, was much dismayed when he heard what Arthur had done, and leaving the tournament, he took the two lads back to the Cathedral and told Arthur to put the sword back in the anvil as he had found it. Then he and Kay tried to draw it out again, but for all their pulling they could not move it an inch.

Then Ector turned to Arthur, who stood by them wondering.

'See if you can pull it out again,' the knight said.

'That will not be difficult,' said Arthur. And he laid hold of the sword and drew it from the anvil again just as easily as he had done before.

Then Sir Ector and Kay dropped on their knees before him as he stood there with the sword in his hand, and hailed him king of England.

HOW ARTHUR CAME TO HIS KINGDOM

'Why do you kneel to me, my own dear father and brother?' cried Arthur in distress, for even now he did not know that he was not really Sir Ector's younger son.

'Nay, my lord Arthur, I was never your father, though I never guessed you were of such high blood,' said the good old knight. And he told Arthur how Merlin had brought him to him when he was a tiny baby; and how he and his wife had brought the little fellow up as their own child, determined that he should never miss his own parents, whoever they might be.

Arthur was filled with sorrow when he learnt that the good knight whom he loved so dearly was not his father. But he was not given time to mourn long. Sir Ector took him at once to the Archbishop and the Archbishop sent for all the nobles to come to the Cathedral again, and there, in front of them all, Arthur drew the sword from the anvil.

But the great nobles were angry that a boy so young as Arthur, whose birth no one knew, should be king over them. And they refused to receive the sign.

'We will come again at Candlemas,' they said, as they mounted their horses and rode away.

'Perchance by then one will be found more worthy to be our king.'

So at Candlemas there was another great gathering, but though all the nobles tried their hardest to draw the sword, none might move it until Arthur laid his hand upon its hilt. Then again it came at his pull as lightly and easily as though it had never been stuck fast in the stone. Yet still the nobles would not accept such a boy for their king.

'We will pray to God again,' they said. And twice more, at Easter and Pentecost, they made other trials. But none of them might move the sword save Arthur, and at last the common people, who had heard of the miracle with awe, and who had watched the trials eagerly, would be held back no longer.

'It is God's will that Arthur should be king—we will have Arthur for our king,' they cried. And the great lords and nobles were obliged to give in.

They knelt down before Arthur and begged him to forgive them for doubting him so long. And then Merlin came forward and told them who the boy really was, and all the people were glad when they heard that he was Uther's son. Then

HOW ARTHUR CAME TO HIS KINGDOM

Arthur was made a knight, and after that the Archbishop crowned him king of England, and the sword was laid upon the high altar for a gift to God.

And that is the way in which Arthur, who, as Merlin had foretold to Vortigern long ago, was to be the greatest king that ever reigned in England, came at last to his kingdom.

THE SWORD EXCALIBUR

AFTER he had been made king, Arthur's first duty was to free the country from the hordes of savage tribes that were invading it. For the first few years of his reign, all his time was spent in war, and the nobles who had been doubtful about making him their king soon changed their way of thinking. For he was so brave and eager and enthusiastic himself that he inspired all his men with courage and determination. And they fought for him so bravely that very soon he succeeded in freeing the land of his enemies, and his people were able to live in peace and quietness again.

Then, when the fighting was over, Arthur gathered his knights to his court at Camelot, and there, helped by Merlin's wise counsels, he set himself to the business of ruling his country well. But although they were now at peace, the king and his knights did not neglect their knightly pursuits. Every day they practised with their weapons, and they often held tournaments to test their skill, and soon they became famous all through the world for their bravery at deeds of arms. And whenever a man suffered wrong from another, or was in any distress or danger, he would come to Arthur's court and ask for help; and Arthur or one of his knights would ride out and do battle for him against those who oppressed him and see that his wrongs were righted. Many were the ladies in distress whom the king and his knights rescued, and many unhappy prisoners did they set free.

One day there came to the court a squire mounted upon horseback, bearing before him a knight who was so badly wounded that he was dying. The squire told the king that not far away, in a great forest, a strange knight had set up a tent beside a well, and would allow no man to pass by that way unless he would joust with him.

'My master gave battle to him,' said the squire, 'and now he is slain. I pray that you will avenge his death.'

Then Arthur was very angry, and he swore that justice should be done to the dead knight, and that one of his own company should ride out and give battle to the stranger.

Now there was in Arthur's court a young squire

named Griflet, and when he heard what Arthur said, he started up and begged the king to knight him and allow him to ride out and do battle with the knight of the well. Arthur did not want to do this, for Griflet was little more than a boy, not nearly old enough to fight against a skilful warrior such as the strange knight appeared to be. But he had made a rule in his court that the man who first asked that he might do any deed of bravery should be given the quest. And so, much against his will, he knighted Griflet upon the spot, and let him ride out to the knight of the well.

But, as might have been expected, Griflet was overcome by the strange knight, and he rode back to court again sorely wounded.

Then Arthur determined that he himself would go and fight against the stranger. He said no word to his nobles, but he told his servants to call him early the next morning before it was day, and to see that his horse and his armour were waiting for him. And while it was still dark, he left the court, alone and unattended, and rode out to avenge the defeat of his young squire.

He thought that no one knew what he meant to do. But Merlin, the wise man, had guessed his intention and, when daylight came, Arthur found the magician riding beside him. Merlin tried to persuade the king not to proceed with the quest.

' He is a great and powerful knight, a king named Pellinore, one of the best knights-at-arms in the world,' he said, and he did his best to make the king turn back. But Arthur would not be persuaded, and when they came to the place where the strange knight had set up his tent, he challenged him at once to do battle with him.

Then the two kings rode full-tilt at each other, and a great contest took place. Arthur was a brave and skilful fighter, but he soon found that Merlin had spoken truly, and that he was indeed no match for the stranger. Very soon he was unhorsed and brought to the ground. Then the stranger knight leapt from his horse and attacked the king with his sword, and, after a fierce struggle, he dealt such a powerful blow that Arthur's sword broke in two, so that he was left helpless at the mercy of the opponent.

The stranger knight dropped his sword.

' Now yield thee to me, Sir Knight,' he said courteously, but Arthur, furious at having been overcome would not listen to him. All unarmed as he was he rushed at the knight and seized him with his naked hands and threw him to the ground. But even when it came to wrestling, the stranger was a better man than the king, and soon he had Arthur at his mercy again.

Then Merlin, fearing lest the king should be killed, sprang forward.

'Hold thy hand, Sir Knight,' he cried. 'For if you slay that knight you will bring this realm into grievous trouble. He is a man of more worship than you know.'

'Why, who is he?' asked the knight. And Merlin said:

'It is King Arthur.'

The strange knight was grieved when he heard this, but he was more afraid of the king's anger than he was sorry at having overcome him in fair fight. And he drew his sword meaning to kill his fallen opponent, for he feared that if he let the king go he would surely be avenged upon him. But Merlin saw what he was about to do, and using his magic power he cast a spell upon the stranger so that he fell to the ground in a deep sleep.

King Arthur rose quickly to his feet. But when he saw the knight lying on the ground he thought that he was dead, and he was filled with grief that such a brave man should have perished.

'Alas, Merlin! What have you done? You have slain this good knight by your crafts,' he cried. 'I would rather have lost all my possessions than have him die thus, for there is not so worshipful a knight in the whole of my realm.'

'Be not afraid, he is not dead,' said Merlin. 'He is wholer than you are—he is but in a deep sleep from which he will awake in a few hours. I was obliged to cast my spell upon him, otherwise you would have been slain. I told you what a good knight he was, but you would not heed my advice. Now come, let us leave him to recover himself, while we find some one who will heal your hurts.'

Then he took the king to a hermit, who dressed Arthur's wounds and gave him healing medicines to drink. For three days the hermit tended the king, then the wounds were so nearly cured that Arthur and Merlin were able to ride away.

So they set off together, but Arthur was not happy.

'I would I had a sword,' he said. For his own sword having been broken in the battle he had now no weapon at all, and he felt the disgrace keenly.

'There is a sword that shall be yours,' said Merlin. And he took the king to the margin of a broad lake and pointed across its shining surface.

'See,' he said. 'There is the sword.'

Arthur gazed out across the water, and he saw a white arm raised above the lake, grasping a splendid sword in its hand. And walking towards them over the water there came a lady of wonderful beauty.

'It is the Lady of the Lake,' said Merlin. 'She dwells below the water in a marvellous castle. When she comes to us, ask her to give you that sword.'

The Lady of the Lake, as though she knew for what purpose they had come, walked straight across to the shore where Arthur and Merlin were standing. As she drew near, the king saluted her and begged her to give him the wonderful sword.

'It is for you,' said the lady. 'Only see that you give it back to me when the time comes.'

'That will I,' said Arthur fervently. And then the lady told him to get into a small barge that was anchored close by and row out across the water and take the sword from the hand that held it. So Arthur and Merlin dismounted from their horses and tied them to a tree, and stepping into the barge rowed out across the water. And when Arthur had taken the sword the hand and arm disappeared, and they rowed back to land again.

'Which like you the best—the sword or the scabbard?' asked Merlin as they rode away.

'The sword,' said Arthur.

'Then you are unwise,' said the magician. 'Great is the sword Excalibur and marvellous, and many are the battles you shall win with it; but the scabbard is worth ten times the value of the blade. While you wear it you shall never lose blood, be you ever so sorely wounded. Wherefore guard well the scabbard and keep it always upon you when you fight.'

No further adventures befell Arthur and Merlin on that occasion, and very soon they reached the court in safety, where they found all the knights and courtiers very anxious about their king and very glad to see him back again safe and well. But when they heard what he had been doing, they were amazed that he should have ventured alone upon such a dangerous quest.

'The king ought not so to jeopard his person,' they said.

But they loved Arthur all the more for his bravery and daring. And they said one to another that it was good to serve under a king who was not afraid to put himself in danger.

THE ROUND TABLE

NOW that Arthur was old enough to marry, his knights urged him to find himself a wife. But Arthur would not take such an important step without Merlin's advice, so he called the wise man to him and asked for his counsel.

'It is well that you should marry,' said Merlin. 'A man of your greatness should not be without a wife. Now tell me, is there any woman you love more than another?'

'Yes,' answered Arthur eagerly. 'I love Guinevere, the daughter of King Leodegrance of the land of Cameliard. She is the fairest damsel living, and she it is whom I would wish above all others to have for my wife.'

Merlin shook his head doubtfully as the king spoke.

'Truly, Sire,' he said, 'there is no doubt of her beauty. She is certainly one of the fairest ladies alive. But I would that you did not love her. For I could have found you a maiden, as fair as she, with whom you would find greater happiness.'

But Arthur's mind was made up. If he might not marry Guinevere he did not wish to marry anybody. And Merlin, who in his wisdom could look into the hearts of men, saw that it would be no good to try and persuade him to marry any one else. At Arthur's wish, he went with an escort to the court of King Leodegrance, and told him that the King of England desired to wed his daughter.

Leodegrance was delighted when he heard this news. Arthur's fame had gone abroad throughout all lands, and there was no other king in the world who was so brave and honourable.

'It is the best tidings that ever I heard,' said King Leodegrance. And he began at once to make his arrangements to send his daughter to Arthur's court.

'With her I will send a gift that shall surely please the king,' he said to Merlin. 'In my court there is a great table, the Round Table given to me by Arthur's father, Uther Pendragon. A hundred and fifty knights may sit at it when it is full. I will give this for my daughter's dowry, and with it I will send a hundred good knights to be the king's true men and serve him until death.'

THE ROUND TABLE

Then Guinevere was given to Merlin, and the Round Table, attended by its hundred knights, was placed upon a great barge, and the party set out for Arthur's court.

When Arthur heard that Merlin was returning successful from his quest, he was full of joy. He was especially pleased with the gift of the Round Table, and he gladly received into his service the knights who accompanied it.

'This Table is more pleasing to me than any riches or lands,' he said. And he called all his knights together and made them into a great company which he called The Knights of the Round Table. And each knight was given a seat at the Table, and his name was written upon his seat in letters of gold.

But when all the knights had taken their places at the Round Table, there were still three vacant places. The king was rather disturbed at this, but Merlin told him that the places would be filled in good time, when the knights who were worthy to sit there should be found.

Then arrangements were made for the king's wedding, and messengers were sent throughout the land to tell the people of Arthur's coming marriage. And the king sent a declaration by the messengers, saying that if any man had a boon to ask, he should come to his court on the day of the wedding and ask it, and if it were not too unreasonable it should be granted.

Many people took advantage of the king's offer, and Arthur kept his word faithfully and gave them what they asked. Then, when everybody else had been dealt with, there came a poor cowherd into the court, bringing with him a young man, who was mounted upon a very old and lean horse. The young man was tall and strong and handsome, and though he was dressed in rags, he bore himself as though he had been some one of distinction. The cowherd made his way to the king and bowed humbly before him.

'Sire,' he said, 'it has been told me that at the time of your marriage you would give to any man whatsoever gift he might ask, provided it were not unreasonable. I pray you now to grant the boon I crave.'

'You have heard truly, and I will keep my word if it is possible,' said the king. 'What is the gift you crave?'

'It is that this, my foster-son, may be made knight,' said the man.

The king was dismayed. It was one of the rules

of knighthood that no man might be made knight unless he came of good parentage. But yet he felt that he could not break his word.

'It is a hard thing that you ask of me,' he said. And the cowherd answered tremblingly:

'Oh, Sire, I know that it is a hard thing. But it is not my own desire, it is the desire of my foster-son. I have thirteen other sons, and they will all do whatever toil I put them to. But this child will not labour or do any work that I command him. From his earliest childhood he has practised swordplay and the casting of darts, and his one desire and longing is to be made knight. He is of no use to me, and so I have brought him to you in the hope that you may grant my request.'

The king looked at the young man curiously, wondering that the son of a poor cowherd should have taste for knightly pursuits. He was very taken with the young man's appearance, and he spoke to him kindly and asked him his name.

'Sire, my name is Tor,' the young man said. And he held himself so straightly, and spoke in such brave and ringing tones, that Arthur felt his heart go out to him. And he determined to grant his request and make him a knight, no matter what people might say.

'Have you a sword?' he asked. And Tor drew a sword from a scabbard that hung at his side. Then, at Arthur's command, he knelt down at the king's feet and bowed his head. And Arthur smote him on the back of his neck with the sword and said:

'Rise up, Sir Tor. Be you a good knight and true.'

Then he turned to Merlin who was standing by his side.

'Say, Merlin, have I done well to make this poor youth knight?' he asked.

'Yes, Sire, you have done well,' answered the magician. 'And he shall indeed be a good knight and true, for he comes of noble birth. He is not the son of this poor cowherd. He is the son of King Pellinore, a brave and valiant warrior, and his mother delivered him at his birth into the charge of this cowherd, who knew not who the baby was. King Pellinore himself knows not that he has such a goodly son.'

'Tell me where to find this King Pellinore,' cried Arthur, 'and I will send for him and show him, then.'

'He is not far away, indeed you have already met with him,' said Merlin with a smile. 'He it was whom you fought with in the forest, the Knight of the Well. You have reason to know that he is indeed a good knight.'

When Arthur heard that the father of Sir Tor was the stranger knight who had overcome him at the well, he was more pleased than ever to send for him. And when King Pellinore had been brought to the court, he presented Tor to him and told him Merlin's story. King Pellinore was overjoyed to find that he had such a brave and handsome son, and he and Arthur were made friends together.

Then with great ceremony and pomp Arthur's marriage to Guinevere took place, and there were great feastings and rejoicings at Camelot. And Pellinore and his son Tor became King Arthur's knights, and two of the vacant places at the Round Table were filled.

THE LAST DAYS OF MERLIN

FOR many years after he was made king, Arthur was helped by the wisdom and counsel of Merlin, the wonderful man who was looked upon as a magician by the people of England, who had prophesied the coming of Arthur, and had done so much to help him gain his kingdom. But for all his wisdom and cleverness, Merlin sometimes did foolish things, and towards the end of his life he did a very foolish thing indeed. He fell deeply in love with a lady of great beauty who practised magic arts herself, and he put himself so completely into her power that at last she was able to bring his life to an end.

This lady did not love Merlin at all, but she let him think that she did because she wanted him to tell her some of the secrets of his great power. And Merlin let her coax from him many of the secrets of his magic power.

But although he was acting so foolishly, Merlin still kept his wonderful power of seeing into the future, and he knew quite well that some evil would soon befall him. And knowing that his time on earth was nearly ended, he gave Arthur much wise counsel and told him many things which would help him after he himself was gone.

'For I shall not be with you much longer,' the old magician said. 'I know that my end is drawing near—some great trouble will soon come upon me. But you have many years to live and reign, and if you follow my counsel, great shall your glory be. But of one thing I warn you most solemnly —keep guard over your sword Excalibur and the scabbard, for they will be stolen from you by a woman. But peradventure you shall find them again, and while you have them both you will always conquer in battle.'

Arthur was very distressed when he heard Merlin's gloomy forebodings.

'Since you know so well of your coming misfortune, why do you not use your magic arts to ward off the trouble ?' he asked.

But Merlin shook his head.

'That may not be,' he said with a sigh. 'To all men there comes an end of life, and though I be wiser than most men, yet I may not use my wisdom to put death away from me. But pay heed to my words now, for after I am gone you shall miss me sorely.

Soon after this, the lady with whom Merlin was in love left the court. Merlin went with her, much to her annoyance. She was growing very tired of the old wizard, and she was making all sorts of plans in her mind to get rid of him. But she did not let Merlin see that she was angry with him for following her. There were still many magical things she wished to know, and she made use of her power over him to coax them from him.

But there was one secret Merlin would not tell her for a long tine.

'You who are so wise and wonderful, how shall you come to die?' she asked him, for she knew that death in its ordinary form could have no power over this great enchanter. 'Is there any way in which you might meet with your end?'

'Yes,' said Merlin, 'there is one way.'

But he still would not tell her what that way was.

The lady, however, was determined to discover it. She had learnt all Merlin's secrets now, except this, and she made up her mind to learn this one too, in order that she might get rid of her troublesome lover. And at last, one day, Merlin gave in to her and told her all that she wanted to know.

'Close here,' he said, 'there is a magic rock into which it is ordained that I shall one day enter, nevermore to come out.'

'Have you ever been inside?' asked the lady.

'Yes,' said Merlin, 'for I know the enchantment that will open it to me. But there is an enchantment that will shut it for all time. And one day I shall be imprisoned in it for evermore.'

'Ah, show me that rock?' begged his companion. And Merlin took her and showed her the rock beneath which he was one day fated to sleep.

Then she begged him to show her how the rock opened, and once more Merlin gave in to her. He even took her inside to show her the marvels of this underground cavern. But the lady had learnt more magic than Merlin realised, and while he was still within the rock, she slipped outside and cast a spell upon it that caused it to shut fast for ever.

Then she went away, leaving Merlin to sleep beneath the enchanted stone. But the old magician had lived a long and weary life, and had seen many sad and sorrowful things, and so perhaps after all he was glad to be at rest at last.

SIR LANCELOT OF THE LAKE

OF all the knights of King Arthur's court, there were none so brave and gallant as Sir Lancelot of the Lake. In tournament and joust and deeds of arms he surpassed all other men; and though he rode out on more dangerous quests, and fought more battles than any other of the Knights of the Round Table, he was never overcome unless it was by treachery or by some enchantment.

Arthur loved and trusted Lancelot above all his knights, and Lancelot served the king very loyally and faithfully, all the more so because he was in love with the king's wife, Guinevere. He could not marry her, of course, because she was already Arthur's wife; but he worshipped her in his heart above every other woman in the world. And he made a vow that he would never marry any other woman, since he might not marry her, but would keep himself loyal and faithful to Guinevere all his life long.

And all the adventures he rode upon, and all the quests he undertook, and all the great battles he fought, he did them all for Guinevere's sake. When his opponents yielded to him in battle, he sent them to swear allegiance to Guinevere as the price of their lives; when he won prizes in the tournaments in which he jousted, he gave them all to Guinevere; and he was always ready to fight for her honour against any knight in the world. And he used to say that it was his great love for the queen that gave him his strength in battle, and that so long as he fought for her he could never be beaten.

One day, Sir Lancelot and another knight of Arthur's court, named Lionel, rode out together in search of adventures. It was a hot day and both the knights were fully armed, and as the afternoon drew on, Lancelot especially was filled with a great desire to sleep. As they rode, they came to a tall apple tree growing in a hedge, and Sir Lionel said: 'Let us rest ourselves and our horses in the shadow of this tree for a little while.'

Lancelot was only too glad to do this. So the two knights dismounted and tied their horses up in the shade of the apple tree; and then Lancelot flung himself down on the cool grass, and, half-hidden in the shadow of the hedge, fell sound asleep. Sir Lionel sat beside him, lazily watching him while he slept, and as he watched he saw three knights riding fast in the distance. They seemed to be fleeing from another knight, who was very big and powerful, and as Sir Lionel rose to his feet in order to see them better, he saw the fourth knight overtake the three in front and overcome them one by one. And when he had overthrown them, he bound them fast with their own bridles and flung them face downwards across their horses' backs.

Sir Lionel was filled with indignation when he saw the way the big knight was treating his captives. For all the knights of Arthur's court were trained to show great courtesy and kindness to their conquered enemies.

'That knight needs a lesson in chivalry,' he thought to himself. And without waking Lancelot, he mounted his horse and rode quickly after the knight, who was disappearing in the distance.

'This adventure shall be mine, not Lancelot's,' he said, and he shouted to the big knight to stop that he might do battle with him. This the stranger knight was nothing loth to do; but he was much stronger and much more powerful than the knight of the Round Table, and he soon overcame Sir Lionel. Then he treated him as he had treated his other captives. He bound him tightly, hand and foot, and flinging him upon his horse's back, led him away with the other three knights to his castle. When they reached the castle he took away all their armour and beat them cruelly, and then shut them up in a dark dungeon amongst many other unfortunate captives.

But Lancelot, knowing nothing of what was happening to Sir Lionel, lay sleeping under the apple tree. And while he slept four queens rode by that way. They were mounted upon milk-white mules, and beside them rode four knights, who held a cloth of green silk aloft on the points of their spears to shield the queens from the heat of the sun. As the cavalcade passed by the apple tree, Lancelot's horse neighed, and the riders saw the knight in armour lying on the ground.

The four queens stopped to look at the knight who lay so peacefully sleeping, careless of what dangers might befall him as he lay. Now Lancelot had taken off his helmet, and when the queens saw his face they knew at once who he was, for his fame had gone abroad in many lands. He looked very brave and gallant as he lay there, and all four of the queens were attracted by the famous knight, and each of them wished that he would fall in love with her, and pay her the homage and devotion that he gave to Queen Guinevere. And they began to squabble amongst themselves a little as to which of them might gain his love.

One of the four queens was Morgan le Fay, King Arthur's half-sister. She was skilled in magic arts, and very wise and clever as well, and she knew that the only way of winning Lancelot's love would be by guile.

'Let us not strive with one another,' she said to the other three queens. 'We cannot all have him, and if we wake him with our quarrelling none of us will. I tell you what we will do. I will put an enchantment upon him so that he will sleep for many hours, and carry him away to my castle. And when once we have him safely under lock and key, I will take away the enchantment from him, and tell him that he shall never regain his freedom unless he will swear allegiance to one of us. He himself shall choose which of us it shall be, thus much free-will shall we allow him.'

The other three queens agreed to this plan. They knew that if Lancelot were to awake before he was safely in their power, he would never swear allegiance to any of them. For all the world knew of his great love for Guinevere, and how he had pledged himself to love and serve no other woman save King Arthur's queen. And they knew, too, that he was quite strong enough and brave enough to overthrow all their attendants if they should try to hold him against his will. So Morgan le Fay threw a spell upon him so that he might not wake. And then the four knights laid him upon his shield and carried him into her castle.

When Lancelot awoke at last from his enchanted sleep, he found himself lying upon the floor in a cold chamber, bare and empty, with no comfort of any kind within it. As he raised himself upon his elbow and looked around him, wondering where he was and how he had come there, a maiden unlocked the door of his prison and came into the room, bringing him something to eat. Lancelot begged her to tell him where he was, but the maiden shook her head.

'Sir, I can tell you nothing now,' she said. And she hurried out of the room and the door was locked behind her.

All that night Lancelot lay on the bare floor of the empty chamber. There was no way of escape, for the door was fast locked and the windows were

They hailed Arthur as the king of England.

Page 18

The Lady of the Lake walked straight across to the shore.

Page 27

heavily barred, and all the knight's armour and weapons had been taken from him so that he was helpless in the hands of his captors. Nobody came near him the next morning until nearly midday, and then the four queens, dressed in their richest robes, came into his prison cell.

'Sir Knight,' said Morgan le Fay, 'we have brought you here because we know that you are the noblest knight living, and because we all covet your love. We know that you have sworn to serve no other woman save Queen Guinevere, but now that you are our prisoner no man will think ill of you if you break your vow. For unless you choose one of us and swear that you will give her the allegiance you have vowed to Guinevere, you shall stay in this prison till you die. Therefore choose—which of us will you have ?'

But if they thought that Lancelot would be frightened by their threats, they little knew him. He threw his head back proudly as he stood before them.

'Sooner will I die in prison than be false to my lady Guinevere,' he said. And in spite of all the four queens could do or say, that was all the answer he would make them.

At last the queens went away and left Lancelot

alone in his cell once more. They were very angry at his loyalty to Guinevere, and they made up their minds to keep him a prisoner in the little bare room until he should give in to their demands. But the maiden who waited upon Lancelot admired him for his loyalty and bravery, and she was indignant with the queens for keeping such a noble knight a prisoner. She herself was in need of the help of some brave knight, and at last she made up her mind that she would try and help Lancelot to escape out of the power of Morgan le Fay.

So she came into the cell where Lancelot was pacing restlessly up and down.

'Sir,' she said, 'if you will but do as I ask you, I will deliver you out of your distress.'

Lancelot turned to her eagerly when he heard these words.

'Tell me what you ask?' he said. 'Thankful indeed will I be if you deliver me from the hands of these sorceresses.'

Then the maiden told him that her father, who was a king, was in great distress. For another king who was very strong and powerful was making war upon him. The two kings had arranged to hold a tournament upon a certain day, in which each would bring all his knights into the field, and whoever won the tournament should be acclaimed the victor.

'One fight have they had already,' said the maiden. 'And my father's enemy brought with him three knights from Arthur's court to fight for him. Thanks to these knights and their prowess my father was overcome. But I hear from my mistress that you are Sir Lancelot of the Lake, the flower of all the knights in the world, and if you will but fight upon my father's side, the victory will surely be his in the coming battle. Therefore, fair sir, if you will but promise to do battle for my father in the tournament, I will find a way to deliver you out of the hands of these queens.'

'Tell me what is your father's name: then will I give you my answer,' said Lancelot. For not even to save himself from prison or from death, would Lancelot do battle in an unjust cause.

'My father is King Bagdemagus,' replied the maiden, and Lancelot nodded his head in satisfaction.

'I know your father well,' he said. 'He is a good king and a noble knight, and willingly will I fight in his battle.'

Then the maiden made her plans to help Lancelot to escape. And very early the next morning she came to him in his prison before any one else was awake and unlocked the doors that led from the castle cells. She showed him where his armour had been placed and helped him to array himself in it again. Then she took him out to the stables where Lancelot found his horse, and after that she unlocked the gates of the castle and led him outside. Then she told him to ride to an abbey which was not far away and take shelter there with the monks, until she could bring her father to him.

Lancelot did as she told him and rode on through a forest until he reached the abbey, where he waited until King Bagdemagus and his daughter came. King Bagdemagus was overjoyed to think that he would have such a splendid knight to fight for him, and he told Lancelot all the plans he had made for the coming battle.

'Know you who were the knights from Arthur's court who bore arms against you in the last battle?' asked Lancelot.

'They were Sir Mordred and Sir Mador and Sir Gahalantine,' answered the king.

Lancelot was glad to know this, for none of them were amongst his particular friends and companions. If they had been, he would have been sorry to have fought against them. But as it was he had no qualms at all, for he thought that they ought not to have arrayed themselves against a king who was so noble and just as Bagdemagus.

'Sir,' he said to the king, 'I will assuredly fight for you and do my utmost to gain for you the victory. Look now, send to me here at this abbey, three of your best and most trusted knights. Let them carry blank shields in place of their own, and send me also a shield that is blank, that none may know what knights we be. We four will wait in a little wood close to where the tournament shall be held, and hold ourselves in readiness to come to your aid when and where you shall require our assistance.'

The king willingly did as Lancelot suggested; and on the day appointed for the tournament Lancelot and the three knights hid themselves in a little wood and waited for the battle to begin. They soon saw that Bagdemagus was likely to be beaten, for his enemy had twice as many knights in the field as he had, not counting the three knights from Arthur's court. The two parties met together in a wild charge, but Bagdemagus's side met with a bad reverse in the very beginning of the fight. Many of the king's knights were unhorsed, while only a few of the enemy's party fell. It looked as though the battle would very soon be over.

Then, into the very thickest of the fight, rode Lancelot with his three companions, and so bravely and fiercely did they lay about them, that many of the enemy wavered and fell. Lancelot himself bore down five of them at the first stroke of his spear, and within a very short space twelve more were overcome by his efforts alone. Heartened by this unexpected assistance, Bagdemagus's other knights rallied, and soon things began to grow more even. The three knights from Arthur's court, Mordred and Mador and Gahalantine, did their best to unhorse Lancelot. They did not know who he was because of his blank shield, but they saw that he was far the most powerful of their opponents, and each longed for the honour of overthrowing him. But they could not prevail against the great knight, and very soon Lancelot had overcome them all.

At last the other king's knights would fight no longer.

'The stranger knight is too mighty for us,' they cried. And they threw down their arms and would joust no more. And so, thanks to Lancelot, King Bagdemagus won the victory.

The king and his daughter took Lancelot back to their castle and made a great feast in his honour, and thanked him again and again for his help. Lancelot rested there for the remainder of that day and the night. But the next day, although they still wanted to keep him, he would stay no longer.

'I have still to find Sir Lionel, who went from me whilst I slept. I fear that some evil has befallen him,' he said, when they pressed him to remain with them a little longer.

Then, having promised the king and his daughter that he would fight for them again should they ever need him to do so, Lancelot took his leave of them and rode away in search of further adventures.

HOW LANCELOT OVERCAME SIR TURQUINE

ONE day, while Lancelot was still searching for Sir Lionel, he came to a great forest; and as he rode through it he met a maiden riding on a white palfrey, alone and unattended. Lancelot drew rein and saluted her courteously.

'Fair damsel,' he said, 'know you of any adventures in this forest?'

'Yes, Sir Knight,' answered the lady. 'There are great adventures here for the man who is brave enough to prove them.'

'Then I pray you take me to them,' cried Lancelot, eagerly.

The maiden looked at him doubtfully.

'Ah, sir, if you dared fight against the strongest and mightiest knight in the world, I can surely take you to where he is. But I warn you that he is very cruel and strong.'

'That is no matter to me,' said Lancelot with a laugh. 'I am Lancelot of the Lake, and never yet have I been overthrown in fair fight.'

The lady's face brightened when she heard Lancelot's name.

'If indeed you be Lancelot, perhaps you may be able to overcome this knight, whose name is Sir Turquine,' she said. 'If Lancelot of the Lake may not overthrow him, there is surely none that may; great glory will it be to the man who overcomes him, for it is shame to the order of knighthood that he should continue to live. He is fierce and cruel as well as strong; and he keeps shut up in his castle more than three score brave knights whom he has conquered in battle. Many of them are knights from Arthur's court, for he has a special grudge against the company of the Round Table. He lies in wait to overcome them, and when he has taken them captive he treats them with great cruelty. Only a short while ago he carried to his castle four of Arthur's knights, amongst them being Sir Kay and Sir Lionel.'

'Is that so?' cried Lancelot in great indignation. 'Then will I the more willingly go with you. I pray you, lady, lead me at once to this strong knight.'

So the maiden turned her palfrey and rode beside Sir Lancelot. And as they rode along, she told him of another wicked knight who lived close by.

'He is even more wicked than Sir Turquine,'

she said. 'For he lies in wait to rob and hurt ladies who happen to ride by that way. If they be accompanied by knights he leaves them unharmed, for he is too great a coward to dare to meet another knight in open battle. But should they ride alone, then will he fall upon them and take from them all that they possess.'

'False knight must he be indeed—thus to make war upon defenceless women!' said Lancelot. 'What is this recreant fellow's name?'

'He calls himself Sir Peris of the Forest,' answered his companion.

'Then when I have accomplished this first quest, I will ride with you to where this Sir Peris has his abode and destroy him,' Lancelot said.

Very soon Lancelot and his guide came within sight of Sir Turquine's castle. As they drew near the cruel knight himself came in sight, and Lancelot marvelled at his great size and strength. He was riding along towards the castle, driving before him a horse on which a knight in armour was lying, bound and helpless. To his horror, Lancelot recognised the imprisoned knight as Gaheris, one of the Knights of the Round Table; and filled with anger at the sight, he gripped his spear and rode fast towards Sir Turquine, crying out:

LANCELOT AND SIR TURQUINE

'Defend yourself, Sir Turquine. I have come to prove my strength against you for the shame that you have done to the Knights of the Table Round.'

Sir Turquine swung round to meet him with a scornful laugh.

'An you be of the Round Table, I defy you and all your fellowship,' he said. And putting his spear in rest he hurled himself upon Sir Lancelot.

The two knights met together in a dreadful shock of battle. So tremendous was it, that both their horses sank dead beneath them, so that the knights had to continue their fight on foot. Then for two hours they struggled fiercely together, neither of them able to gain any advantage over the other, though they were both dreadfully wounded and exhausted and out of breath. At last they were so worn out that they were obliged to pause and rest for a while.

Turquine looked at Lancelot with grudging admiration.

'You are the best knight that ever I met,' he said. 'I would willingly make peace with you, if you will make peace with me. Let us make a truce together, and because of the splendid fight you have made against me I will set all my prisoners free. Tell me what your name is ? So long as you be not one knight, I would fain be friends with you.'

'Who is the one knight with whom you will not be friends ?' asked Lancelot.

'It is Lancelot of the Lake,' replied Sir Turquine. 'Long years ago he slew my brother in battle, and I have taken a solemn vow to be revenged upon him when we meet. It is because of him that I have made such warfare upon the Knights of the Round Table.'

'But he slew your brother in fair and honourable battle,' said Lancelot. 'It is unknightly of you thus to bear vengeance in your heart.'

'I care not whether it be unknightly or no,' answered Turquine. 'But tell me your name, Sir Knight, that we two may be friends.'

'I am Lancelot of the Lake,' replied Lancelot.

When Turquine heard the name, he grasped his sword again and turned upon him savagely.

'Then shall I never be friends with you!' he cried. 'Defend yourself, Sir Lancelot, for you shall never depart hence until one of us be dead.'

And he flung himself upon Lancelot again and aimed down blow after blow upon him with his mighty sword.

Lancelot had never fought against such a strong

and skilful opponent before. But he was determined not to give way an inch while life remained in his body. And in the end his courage prevailed over the great strength of the other knight. Sir Turquine was overcome and sank down dead upon the ground.

Then Lancelot set Sir Gaheris free, and taking the keys of Sir Turquine's castle from the body of the dead knight, he gave them to Gaheris and asked him to set Sir Turquine's prisoners free.

'I myself am promised to this damsel who hath another quest for me,' he said. 'But in Sir Turquine's castle there are many knights of Arthur's court. I pray you greet them from me, and bid them go to Arthur at Camelot, where I myself shall hope to come at the Feast of Pentecost.'

Then Gaheris gave Lancelot his horse, for Lancelot's own horse had been killed under him early in the battle. And he himself set off towards Sir Turquine's castle, while Lancelot followed the lady to the spot where the false knight Sir Peris, who made war upon helpless women, had his hiding-place in the forest.

When they drew near to the place, Lancelot told his companion to ride on ahead, while he drew back a little. He was afraid that the cowardly knight might refuse to come forth to battle if he rode beside her. So the lady rode on alone, and as soon as Sir Peris saw her, he sprang out of his hiding-place and dragged her roughly from her palfrey. She cried out loudly to Lancelot, and Lancelot, who was only waiting for her call, spurred fast to her aid.

'Traitor to knighthood! Who taught you so to distress ladies and gentlewomen?' he cried indignantly. And he flew upon Sir Peris and struck him such a blow that the cowardly knight fell from his horse, dead.

'Now have you the payment you have long deserved!' said Lancelot, as he stood over Peris's dead body. Then he turned to the maiden and helped her to her saddle again.

'Have you any more adventures for me?' he asked.

'No, sir, not at this time,' said the maiden.

'Then will I bid you farewell,' said Lancelot.

'Farewell, sir,' said the lady. 'God preserve you wherever you may go, for surely you are the greatest and courtliest knight that lives upon this earth.'

Then Lancelot saluted the lady, and rode upon his way.

THE RESCUE OF SIR KAY

AFTER Lancelot had left Sir Gaheris, the latter went at once to the castle of Sir Turquine, and set the prisoners free. He found sixty-four knights shut up in the castle, and they had all been very cruelly treated and were closely fettered and bound. Gaheris loosed them from their bonds, and they crowded round him with joy and thanked him for their liberty. For they thought that it was he who had overthrown the savage knight.

But Gaheris undeceived them.

'Not so,' he said. 'It was Sir Lancelot who overcame him. He had taken me prisoner and was bringing me hither when Lancelot came and rescued me. I saw the whole battle as I lay bound upon my horse's back. Lancelot sends you his greetings and bids you hasten to Arthur's court, where he himself hopes to meet you shortly.'

Then the knights searched through Sir Turquine's castle until they found their armour which he had taken from them, and in Sir Turquine's stables each man found his horse again. As it was now growing late, they determined to sleep in the castle for that one night, and start back for Arthur's court on the morrow. So they ransacked the castle for wine and food and made a great feast in the hall, and spent the evening in merriment and rejoicing.

Amongst the knights who had been Sir Turquine's prisoners was Sir Kay, Arthur's foster-brother, whom Arthur had made his seneschal after he had been crowned king. Sir Kay was not content to remain in safety in the castle for even one night, knowing that Lancelot, who had saved him, was riding alone upon dangerous adventures. So he took his horse that same evening and rode after Lancelot, hoping that he might overtake the brave knight and help him in some of the perilous quests he was always undertaking.

Kay, at first, had an uneventful journey. But after some days he came into a dangerous country, and one evening, as it was growing late, three knights set upon him at once. Sir Kay defended himself bravely, but although he had courage enough, he was no match against the three stranger knights. Far away in the distance Kay could see a light shining, and hoping that it came from a house where he might find refuge, he turned his horse and rode fast towards it, pursued by his three opponents.

Now it happened that the light shone from a house where Lancelot himself had taken shelter for the night. Lancelot had just lain down to rest, when there came a great knocking at the gate, and hearing the noise he rose up and looked out of his window. There he saw a knight fighting a desperate battle against three other knights, and his heart was stirred within him at the sight. He seized such of his armour as lay within his reach, and taking the sheet from his bed, he threw one end of it out of the window and let himself down by it. Then, sword in hand, he ran to the aid of the knight by the gate, whom, even in that dim light, he recognised as Sir Kay.

The three strange knights turned upon Lancelot fiercely, thinking soon to dispose of this daring man who came against them half-armed. But in spite of his lack of armour, they were no match for Lancelot. Within six strokes, Lancelot had brought them all three to the ground, so that they cried out in amazement to him to spare their lives.

'Save us, and we will yield ourselves to you,' they said.

But Lancelot would not accept their submission.

'*I* have no quarrel with you,' he said. 'It is to this knight, Sir Kay, that you must yield yourselves if you would have me spare your lives.'

The three knights did not much relish doing this.

'We should soon have overcome Sir Kay had it not been for you,' they said. 'Nay, Sir Knight, it is to you and none other that we will yield ourselves.'

But Lancelot was firm.

'If you will that I should save you, you must yield yourselves to Sir Kay. Choose now, whether you will die or live,' he said.

Seeing there was no help for it, the three knights yielded themselves to Sir Kay. Then Lancelot told them to go to Arthur's court and give themselves up to the queen, and tell her that Sir Kay had sent them to swear allegiance to her and do her honour. The three knights took their swords and swore upon them a vow that they would do as Lancelot said; and then they rode away, very subdued and humbled at having been overcome by a half-armed man.

Lancelot took Sir Kay up to the house and roused the host, who let them in and gave them food and wine. As soon as they came into the light, Sir Kay recognised Lancelot, and falling upon his knees before him he poured out his thanks to him for having twice saved him from death. But Lancelot made light of what he had done.

'I have done nothing but what I ought to do,' he said. 'You are welcome to what little service I have been able to give you. Now let us eat and drink, and after that you shall sleep and rest yourself.'

The two knights sat down to the food which the host had brought them, and when they had eaten they lay down together in Lancelot's bed. But Lancelot rose up very early in the morning, while Sir Kay was still sleeping, and he dressed himself in Kay's armour, leaving his own armour and weapons for Sir Kay. He thought that if Kay wore his armour, every one would think that he was Lancelot, and so he would reach home in safety, for people would hesitate to attack him if they thought he was the Knight of the Lake. Lancelot knew that Sir Kay was not a very skilful fighter, and he was afraid lest some unscrupulous knight might do battle with him, hoping to have an easy victory, if he wore his own armour.

Then Lancelot, without waking Sir Kay, went softly downstairs, and saying good-bye to his host, he took his horse and rode away.

THE CHAPEL PERILOUS

SO, clad in Sir Kay's armour, Lancelot set out once more in search of brave adventures. He was not long in finding them, for he had only ridden a very little way when he saw four of Arthur's knights resting under a tree. They were Sir Gawaine and Sir Uwaine and Sir Sagramour and Sir Ector de Maris, and when they caught sight of Lancelot in Kay's armour they thought it was Sir Kay himself.

'By my faith, here comes Sir Kay! I will ride out and prove his might,' cried Sir Sagramour, and he took his spear in his hand and mounted his horse and rode out against the coming knight. The other knights watched him smilingly, for they knew that though Sir Kay was a valiant knight at heart, he was not a very skilful one when it came to deeds of arms.

Lancelot laughed when he saw Sir Sagramour coming to meet him, for he guessed that the knight thought he had an easy victory before him. Spear in rest, he met the onslaught of his opponent, and, to Sir Sagramour's astonishment, he bore him from his horse at the very first stroke.

The other three knights were amazed, and Sir Ector caught up his spear and galloped towards the knight in Kay's armour. But he met with no better luck than Sir Sagramour, and at the first blow he found himself stretched upon the ground.

'It cannot be Sir Kay,' said Uwaine then. 'It must be some savage knight who has overcome and killed him and has taken his armour. I will go out and give battle to him and be avenged upon him for what he has done to Sir Kay.' And he rode fiercely at Lancelot, not to joust with him in friendliness, but with the intention of killing him.

But Lancelot was as easily able to parry his fierce blows as he had been able to parry the friendly blows of Ector and Sagramour. And without doing him any serious injury, he gave him such a stroke that Uwaine reeled from his saddle and fell on the earth.

Then Sir Gawaine took his shield and spear and rode out grimly to be revenged upon his brother knights. But yet a fourth time did Sir Kay's spear gain Lancelot the victory, and having disposed of Gawaine almost as easily as he had done of the other three, the knight rode on his way without waiting for further parley.

'God give him joy who made this spear,' he said to himself. 'Never came there a better one into my hand!' And with a smile at the thought of the four discomfited knights he had left behind him, he urged his horse on to greater speed.

Sir Gawaine and the other three knights picked themselves up from the ground and sorted out their horses, and rode very ruefully back to Arthur's court. But Lancelot went on his way deeper into the forest, hoping to meet with some dangerous adventure.

After he had ridden some way he met a maiden walking in the forest, who was crying and wringing her hands, and seemed to be in some great distress. As soon as she caught sight of Lancelot she recognised him for the great knight of the Round Table, and she greeted him eagerly.

'Oh, Sir Knight, Sir Lancelot! Glad am I to meet with you!' she cried. 'I pray you on your knighthood help my brother, who lies sorely wounded and is likely to die unless some good knight will save him.'

Lancelot, who was always ready to help a lady

in distress, pulled up his horse at once and bent to speak to the maiden.

'Who is your brother, and what can I do to help him ?' he asked.

'My brother is Sir Meliot,' answered the maiden. 'He has been grievously wounded in battle so that I fear lest he should die. I have been to a sorceress who dwells near here, praying her to come and heal him. But she says that my brother may not be healed unless I can find a knight who is brave enough to go into the Chapel Perilous and bring away the sword of a dead knight who lies there, and a piece of the cloth in which his body is wrapped.'

'Gladly will I help you,' answered Lancelot. 'Sir Meliot is a knight of the Round Table, therefore fellowship requires me to render him what aid I can. Tell me where the Chapel Perilous is, and I will ride thither at once and see if I may not achieve this quest.'

'Ah, Sir Knight, but it is a dreadful and dangerous adventure upon which I send you,' said the maiden fearfully. Then she told Lancelot that a dreadful enchantment lay upon the Chapel. It was guarded by thirty tremendous men in black armour, all of whom were far bigger and stronger than any mortal knight. No human being had ever yet entered the Chapel and come out of it alive.

But Lancelot was not frightened by this dreadful tale.

'I am a Christian knight,' he said, 'and I fear no deeds of magic. Take me to this chapel, and if God wills I shall achieve the quest.'

The maiden brought him within sight of the chapel, and then she stood still.

'Here will I wait for you should you return alive,' she said. And she watched tremblingly while Lancelot rode boldly up to the chapel gate.

When he reached the gate, the knight dismounted from his horse and tied it up close by. Then, unsheathing his sword, he walked into the chapel yard. And there he saw the thirty men-at-arms, just as the maiden had said. They were all dressed in black armour, and they towered above Lancelot so that they made him look like a little man beside them. Their faces were very horrible to look at, and when they saw the knight they gnashed their teeth at him and glared at him ferociously.

Lancelot, for all his bravery, could not help feeling a little afraid when he saw these terrible-looking men. But, as he had told the maiden, he was a Christian knight, and he trusted in God to deliver him from danger. He was determined to enter the chapel, and he strode boldly up to the men-at-arms, ready to give them battle. But as he came up to them they scattered before him on every side, so that the way into the chapel lay open before him.

Much encouraged by this, Lancelot went into the Chapel Perilous. It seemed very dark and dim to him at first, for there was only one small light burning inside. But when he had grown a little used to the dimness, he saw the body of a dead knight lying before the altar. The knight was wrapped round with a cloth of fine silk, and a sword lay by his side.

Then Lancelot went up to the altar, and cut away a piece of the silken cloth with his sword. As he did so the floor of the chapel shook as though there had been an earthquake, and Lancelot clutched his sword tightly and paused to see what would happen. But he still kept in his hand the piece of the cloth which he had cut off. And when the ground had grown still again, he took up the sword that was lying beside the dead knight and went out of the chapel.

Outside in the chapel yard he found the thirty men-at-arms drawn up to meet him, looking even more fierce and terrible than before. When Lancelot appeared at the door they all cried out with loud voices:

'Lay down that sword, Sir Knight, else shall you die!'

'I will lay it down for no word of yours,' said Lancelot. 'Fight for it, an you will have it.' And, remembering how they had given way to him before when he had walked boldly up to them, he marched towards them again.

And again the men scattered before his face, leaving him a free passage to the gate.

But when Lancelot reached the gate, a lady suddenly stood in the way before him, and stayed him with uplifted hand.

'Lay down that sword, Sir Lancelot,' she said, 'or you shall surely die.'

But Lancelot grasped the sword still tighter in his hand.

'I leave it not,' he said. And nothing the lady could say would move him.

Then the lady suddenly changed her tone.

'Lancelot, you have won,' she said sweetly. 'If you had put down that sword you would have died. But now my power over you is ended, and I must let you go free. Therefore, to show that you bear me no malice, I pray you give me one kiss before you go.'

But Lancelot lifted his head proudly.

'All my love is vowed to Queen Guinevere, and even my kisses may I not give to any other woman,' he said. And he strode past the lady and mounted his horse again and rode away. And well for him was it that he had the strength to withstand her subtle arts. For the lady was a wicked enchantress, and had he given her even the one kiss she craved he would have put himself in her power. And then his adventures would have been over for ever, and he would have ridden no more upon knightly quests!

When Sir Meliot's sister saw Lancelot riding back to her, bearing in his hand the sword and the piece of cloth from the Chapel Perilous, she wept with joy and relief. She had never thought that he would accomplish his errand, and she had mourned him for dead. She took him to the castle where her brother lay, and when Lancelot saw Sir Meliot lying on a couch, so weak and white that he seemed to be dying, he was filled with pity. He hurried to the wounded knight's side, and touched his hurts with the sword he had brought from the Chapel Perilous. Then, very gently, he wiped them with the silken cloth. And in a moment, as though by some miracle, Sir Meliot was made whole, and he sprang to his feet, as sound and well as he had ever been in his life.

The brother and sister flew into each other's arms, overwhelmed with joy. They were full of gratitude to Lancelot who had brought them this great happiness. They entertained him that night with the best that they had, and thanked him again and again for having saved Meliot's life. They wanted the brave knight to stay with them for awhile and rest from his adventures, but the next day Lancelot took his leave of them and rode away.

'I go to Arthur's court for the feast of Pentecost,' he said. 'Go you there too, and there by the grace of God you shall see me again.'

Then Lancelot rode back to Camelot, where the king and his court were eagerly awaiting his coming. The fame of his great deeds was growing greater day by day, for almost every day some of the knights and ladies whom Lancelot had helped returned to their homes, bringing fresh news of Lancelot's bravery and gentleness and courtliness. And when at last the hero himself appeared, everybody hurried to greet him.

As soon as they saw him in Kay's armour,

Gawaine and his three companions recognised Lancelot for the strange knight who had overthrown them so easily, and they laughed and made merry with each other over the jest that had been played upon them. Then Sir Kay himself appeared, and told the court how Lancelot had left him his own armour so that he might travel home in safety, and how he had twice saved his life. And then Sir Meliot and his sister arrived at the court and told of the brave way in which Lancelot had gone to the Chapel Perilous to bring away the precious things which alone might save Meliot's life. And many others came and told of Lancelot's gallant deeds, and everybody, high and low, paid honour to him.

And so Lancelot's fame spread into all countries, so that he had the greatest name of any knight in the world.

Lancelot lay sleeping under the apple tree.

Page 46

Lancelot was determined to enter the Chapel Perilous.

Page 76

THE SAD STORY OF SIR TRISTRAM

SIR TRISTRAM was one of the bravest and most gallant of all the knights who lived in King Arthur's days. But his story is a very sad one. His mother died when he was born, and his very name has a sad meaning. It means 'The sorrowful born child,' and all through his life sadness seemed to follow him.

When he was about seven years old, his father, King Meliodas, married again, and the new queen was very unkind to her little stepson Tristram. She was very jealous of him because he would inherit his father's lands, and in order that her own sons might have them instead, the wicked queen made a plot to poison the little boy. Twice did she try to take his life, but each time, by a miracle, Tristram was saved, and in the end King Meliodas discovered her wicked plan. The king was dreadfully angry when he found out how cruelly she had behaved to his little son, and he condemned her to be burnt to death.

But when Tristram heard of the terrible sentence passed upon the queen he was very distressed. Boy though he was, he determined to save her if he possibly could, and he went to his father and kneeling down before him, begged of him a boon.

King Meliodas looked at him affectionately.

'Ask what you will, my son, and I will grant it you,' he said.

'Then give me the life of the queen, my stepmother,' Tristram besought him. And though the king was very unwilling to grant this request he could not refuse the boy's pleading. But though the queen's life was spared, the king would not leave his young son in her care any longer. So Tristram was sent away over the sea into a foreign country, to be brought up amongst strangers, far away from all those who were near and dear to him. And it was not until he was almost grown up that he was allowed to come to his own home again.

But at last, when Tristram had learnt all that there was to be learnt in the country over the seas, his father sent for him to come back to his own land once more. And Tristram came, tall and strong and handsome, well skilled in deeds of arms and able to speak foreign languages, and to play the harp better than any one in his own country. He was very glad to see his father again, and he began to long for the time when he should be knighted and able to take his place amongst the knights of Arthur's court, to earn fame and honour in adventures.

He had not long to wait before adventures came his way. His father's brother, Mark, the king of Cornwall, was in very great distress and trouble at the time. The king of Ireland, whose name was Anguish, claimed Cornwall as a subject state, and every year he exacted the payment of a large sum of money from its king. For seven years King Mark had managed to evade the payment of this tribute money; but in the very year that Tristram came to his home again, King Anguish sent to know why the money had not been paid for such a long time. And he ordered that the whole of the payment for the last seven years should be given to his messenger.

King Mark, who was always very brave when danger was far away, sent a message of defiance to the king of Ireland.

'Tell your master if he will have tribute of us that he must send and fight for it,' he said. And he sent the messengers away.

When the king of Ireland received this bold defiance he was very angry, and he sent his wife's brother, who had been knighted by King Arthur and who was the bravest of all the knights at the Irish court, to demand the tribute money from King Mark, and, if need be, fight for it. This knight, whose name was Sir Marhaus, came with a fleet of ships to Cornwall and anchored off the coast and sent a message to King Mark, saying:

'Pay the money that you owe to my lord, the king of Ireland, or else find a champion that shall defend your cause against me.'

Then King Mark was in a great difficulty. He could neither pay the money that he owed, nor could he find a champion to do battle for him. For he was a treacherous and deceitful king, and no great or famous knight would fight for any cause of his; while lesser knights, who might perhaps have fought for a reward, were too afraid of the great skill and fame of Sir Marhaus to venture to ride out against him.

Every day Sir Marhaus sent messengers to King Mark demanding the payment of the tribute money, but, though the king was ashamed and humiliated by the messages the Irish knight sent, he could find no one to be his champion.

At last the news of King Mark's trouble came to the court of King Meliodas, Tristram's father.

THE SAD STORY OF SIR TRISTRAM

Young Tristram was very indignant when he heard of the shame that was being brought upon his family through his uncle's cowardice. And he went in hot haste to his father.

'Sir, give me leave to ride to my uncle and do battle in his cause against this Irish knight?' he cried.

King Meliodas was very distressed when he heard his son's request. He tried to persuade Tristram to abandon his idea, for he knew how brave and strong the knight from Ireland was, while Tristram was only an untried boy. But Tristram would not be persuaded, and at last the king realised that it would not be right to keep him back since he wished so much to go.

'You must do as your own courage tells you,' he said. And Tristram, overjoyed at this permission, poured out his thanks to his father and rode away to Cornwall.

When he reached his uncle's court he offered to do battle against Sir Marhaus. And although he was so young, King Mark, who was only too glad to find any sort of a champion, gave him the order of knighthood and sent him out at once against the Irish knight.

The battle was to take place upon a little island,

close to the harbour where the Irish ships were lying. Tristram with his horse and his armour were put into a boat and were ferried over to the island, while all the people of Cornwall gathered on the shore to watch what would happen. When they saw how young their champion was, they were very indignant with King Mark for letting so young a knight fight his battle for him, and they wept and mourned for the brave boy knight, thinking that they would never see him alive again.

Sir Marhaus, too, was very shocked when he saw how youthful his adversary was, and he did his best to persuade Tristram to return and not to undertake the battle. But Tristram was determined to do his best to wipe out the shame his uncle had brought upon his family, and he insisted that the fight should take place as arranged. So Sir Marhaus was obliged to let it go on. But the Irish knight, who was one of the knights of the Round Table, was as chivalrous as he was brave, and he did his best to console the young man for what he thought would be certain defeat for him.

'Since you will do battle with me, I may not gainsay you, young knight,' he said. 'But I make this one condition. If you can withstand three of my strokes, then you may count yourself unbeaten, and may depart hence with no loss of honour.'

Then the two knights rode fiercely at each other. At the first stroke the spear of Sir Marhaus pierced Tristram's side, but the young knight would not give in. Although he was in great pain from his wound, he fought on doggedly, proving that for all his youth he was a match in skill and courage for any well-tried knight. He withstood a great many more than three of his adversary's strokes, and in the end he struck Sir Marhaus such a blow on the head with his sword that the Irish knight could fight no more. He staggered to his ship and was taken on board by his men, leaving Tristram victor on the island.

Sir Marhaus was so sorely wounded that his servants knew that he could not recover, so they took up the anchors of the ships with all speed and sailed back to Ireland. There was a piece of Sir Tristram's sword still in the knight's head where the blade had splintered, and though the surgeons did their best to get it out they could not do so, and Sir Marhaus died very soon after he had reached the Irish court. The queen of Ireland, the brave knight's sister, was very distressed at her brother's death. She made the surgeons take the piece of the sword out of his head after he was dead, and she put it away carefully, and swore to be revenged upon Sir Tristram if ever it was in her power to do so.

Meanwhile Tristram had been taken back to his uncle's court, very ill himself from the wound Sir Marhaus had given him. Everything possible was done for him, but he grew ever weaker and weaker, until it seemed as though he too must die. At last King Mark sent for a wise woman who knew magic and asked her advice, and she told him that his nephew could never recover so long as he stayed in his own land.

'He must go into the country whence the spear that wounded him came, else may he never be healed,' she said.

When King Mark heard this, he made up his mind that Tristram should be sent to Ireland. A ship was made ready and Tristram was carried on board, and then, attended by faithful servants, he set sail for Ireland. And so that it might not be known who he was, his name was changed to Tramtrist.

Tristram had brought his harp with him in the ship, and as he lay on his bed he passed the long hours away playing upon it. When the ship drew near to Ireland, the people came to listen to the wonderful music he made upon his harp, and the news was brought to the king and queen that there was a wounded man come to Ireland who could play better than any harper who had ever been heard before.

The king and queen were staying in a castle by the seashore, close to the place where Tristram's ship had come to land. The king sent and had the sick man carried up to the castle, and when he heard that he was a wounded knight he gave him into his daughter's care, and charged her to do her best to restore the young man to health again. For his daughter, whose name was Isolde, was very skilful in nursing sick and wounded people.

And under her tender care, Tristram, or Tramtrist as he was known at the Irish court, grew well and strong again as the wise woman's prophecy had foretold.

Isolde was young and very lovely to look upon. So fair was she that she was known as Isolde the Beautiful. She was as good as she was fair, and Tristram fell deeply in love with her, a love which Isolde was not long in returning. Indeed, few people could be long with the handsome and gallant young knight without learning to love him, for

Tristram was one of those people who gain love wherever they go. For a short time the two lovers were very happy together—it was perhaps the only really happy time that Tristram ever knew. He taught his young nurse to play upon the harp, and many happy hours the two would spend, making music and singing songs to each other.

But their happiness was not to last very long. A Saracen knight, whose name was Sir Palomides, came to the court of King Anguish, and as soon as he saw the king's fair daughter he fell in love with her and wished to marry her. He showered gift after gift upon Isolde, and Tristram soon grew full of envy of the man who could declare his love so openly. He himself might not breathe a word of the great longing that possessed him, for if he had asked the king for his daughter's hand in marriage, Anguish would have been sure to have demanded from him an account of his lineage and descent, and then he would have had to have owned that it was he who had caused the death of Sir Marhaus, who was still mourned by everybody at the Irish court.

Very soon after Sir Palomides came to court, King Anguish made a great tournament in his honour, and all his knights came to joust at it.

But they were none of them so skilful as the Saracen knight, and Sir Palomides on the first day overthrew all who came against him. But Tristram was not inclined to let his rival win all the honours, and although he was scarcely healed of his wound, he entered into the lists himself on the second day of the trial. And he fought and overthrew Sir Palomides, and made him swear that he would never disturb Isolde with his attentions again.

Isolde loved the young knight more than ever after he had thus fought so bravely for her. But she was not to have much more happiness with him. One day, the queen, her mother, saw Tristram's sword lying in his chamber, and, picking it up idly, she noticed that a small piece was broken from the blade. At once she remembered the piece of steel that had been taken from her dead brother's head, and filled with suspicion she hurried to her own room and sought in her coffer until she had found it. Then she ran back to Tristram's chamber and fitted the piece that she had treasured against the gap in Tristram's sword, and it filled it exactly.

Then the queen's fury rose against Tristram. Snatching up the sword in her hand she rushed in search of the young knight, and would have killed him on the spot had not one of Tristram's attendants caught her in his arms and pulled the sword from her hand.

But after that Tristram could no longer stay in the castle where he had been so happy. The Irish king sent for him and told him that he must at once depart from his land.

'I do not blame you for defending your country,' King Anguish said. 'You did as a brave knight should, and it is great honour to you that you so well maintain your quarrel. But I may no longer keep you in my palace. Therefore, Sir Tristram, you must return whence you came.'

So Tristram went to Isolde and took his leave of her. Isolde wept bitterly when he said good-bye, and she cried out passionately that she would always be true to him. And Tristram took a solemn vow that he would be faithful to her and fight for no other lady all the days of his life. Then very sorrowfully he went down to his ship and sailed away, leaving his heart behind him in Ireland.

King Mark and Tristram's father were very glad to see him back again, and they made great feasts and rejoicings for his safe return. But in spite of all the honour that was paid him, Tristram was very sad and lonely. He was always thinking and talking of Isolde, and saying how good and sweet and beautiful she was. And at last King Mark fell in love with the lady from his nephew's description of her, and he made up his mind that he would have her for his wife. And he sent for Tristram and told him that he was going to send him as an ambassador to Ireland to ask for the hand of Isolde the Beautiful.

Tristram was aghast when he heard his uncle's plan. But King Mark's word was law in his own land, and Tristram as a younger member of his family was obliged to obey him, or else be forsworn upon his honour as a knight. And when King Mark commanded him to set out at once and bring Isolde back with him to be his bride, he had to take the ship and the men his uncle provided, and set sail for Ireland.

This time he did not have a very prosperous voyage. Very soon after he had started a great tempest overtook him, and the boat was driven away from the Irish coast and borne back to England again. It came to land close by the castle of Camelot, where King Arthur was holding his court, and Tristram decided to anchor there and set up a pavilion on the shore until the storm should have abated.

While he was waiting for the waves to grow calm,

he heard that King Anguish was at Camelot, having been summoned there by Arthur to account for the death of one of Arthur's knights who had been killed in Ireland. Sir Blamore, a cousin of the knight who had been killed in Ireland, had accused the Irish king of treason, and King Anguish had been ordered to do battle against Sir Blamore, or else to find some other knight to fight for him, to prove that it was by accident and not by design that the knight of the Round Table had met with death.

When Tristram heard this news he hurried to King Anguish and begged him, for the love that he bore his daughter, to allow him to take the quarrel upon himself. King Anguish was overjoyed when he heard the young knight's chivalrous offer. For he himself was growing old, and Sir Blamore was young and strong and a very powerful knight, and there had seemed little chance that the king would be able to prove his innocence. He willingly appointed Tristram to fight for him, and a message was sent to Sir Blamore telling him that a champion had been found who would do battle against him on behalf of the king of Ireland.

When the knights of Arthur's court heard that it was Tristram who had come forward to King

Anguish's aid, they crowded to the field of battle. For Tristram's fame had gone abroad after his battle with Sir Marhaus, and they were all eager to see whether the young knight was as brave and skilful as he was reported to be.

They were not long in finding out. In spite of all that Sir Blamore could do, Tristram overthrew him. And then he stood over him and commanded him to yield himself to him and declare that King Anguish was innocent of the crime laid to his charge.

But although Sir Blamore had been conquered, he was as brave as Tristram himself. He had no fear of death, and he refused to speak the words that would save his life.

'I have sworn to do battle to the death,' he said, 'and I will never gainsay my words or yield me to you.'

When Tristram heard his fallen adversary speak in this manner he was very perplexed and did not know what to do. It seemed a dreadful thing to him to have to slay the other knight in cold blood, and yet the rules of battle required him to do so, or else make him speak the words that would declare the king of Ireland to be innocent. But in spite of all he could say, Blamore remained obstinate, and at last in his perplexity Tristram left the field and walked to the dais where the judges sat watching the conflict, waiting to declare him the victor.

He knelt down before them and begged them to intervene.

'It is shame that this noble knight should be killed,' he said. 'And yet the rules of war demand that I shall slay him since he will not speak the word that will set him free. I pray you of your mercy that you will put aside this hard rule and bid me let Sir Blamore live.'

The judges called the knights who were watching together and consulted with them to know what they should do. And in the end they granted Sir Tristram's request, and Sir Blamore was given his life, even though he would not yield, while the king of Ireland was proclaimed innocent of the murder and allowed to return to his own country.

So King Anguish sailed back to Ireland, taking Tristram with him. And when he reached his court and the queen heard how Tristram had saved his life and vindicated his honour, she forgave him for the death of her brother. Isolde was overjoyed to see her lover again, for the days since Tristram had left her had been sad and lonely for her. But her joy did not last long, for Tristram had to break the news that he had come to ask for Isolde's hand in marriage to his uncle King Mark.

King Anguish did his best to persuade the young knight to marry Isolde himself, but Tristram stood firm in his loyalty to King Mark.

'I may not prove treacherous to my uncle,' he said, and in the end King Anguish gave an unwilling consent to his request.

'Rather than all my lands I would that you married her yourself!' he said. 'I know no man in all the world to whom I would more gladly give her. But since you have saved my life, you have a right to do with her as you wish. Therefore, if you must keep your word to your uncle, take her to be his wife.'

'Sir, I should be forever forsworn in all my vows of knighthood did I not fulfil my word,' Tristram answered. And so poor Isolde was given to him, that he might take her with him over the seas to be his uncle's wife.

The queen of Ireland knew how dearly her daughter loved Tristram, and she knew how sad Isolde's life would be if she were married to a man whom she could not love. So she made a wonderful drink, a love potion, and gave it to the waiting-maid who was to go with Isolde to the strange land.

'I charge you solemnly that on the day my daughter and King Mark are wedded you shall give them this drink, and see that each of them pledges the other from the same cup,' the queen said. 'Then shall my daughter's sorrow be turned to happiness, and she and her husband shall love each other truly all the days of their lives.'

The waiting-woman promised the queen that she would do as she was commanded, and the magic wine was put into a golden bottle and stored carefully away in the cabin on board the ship.

But the queen's plan went sadly astray. One day Tristram and Isolde were alone together in the cabin, and they chanced to find the golden bottle. Neither of them knew anything about the love potion, and Tristram laughed as he took it up.

'Here is some wonderful drink that your waiting-woman keeps for herself,' he said. 'Come, let us pledge one another in her precious wine.' And he poured it into a goblet and drank a deep draught of it and then held the cup for Isolde to drink. And she drank too, and they laughed at each other and said that it was the very best wine they had ever tasted.

But though they knew it not, they had drunk of a draught that would bring them bitter pain and sorrow. For after having tasted of that magic drink, there was no power on earth that could ever change their love. They had loved each other well enough before; but now they were to love more passionately still. And their love was to be to them a bitter hopeless longing, that should never leave them until their lives should end.

Isolde was duly married to King Mark with great pomp and ceremony. But the marriage was fated never to be a happy one. All Isolde's love was given to Tristram, and Tristram loved Isolde so passionately and fiercely in return that to be away from her for long was his greatest grief. In time King Mark grew jealous of his nephew and would have killed him, and Tristram had to go from his court and seek adventures far away. Poor Isolde mourned and wept for him when he was departed, and her husband, angry at her grief, treated her very cruelly, so that Tristram, putting aside all thought of his own danger, came again to King Mark's castle and carried her away.

Then King Mark promised to forgive Tristram if he would bring Isolde back to him. And he said that Tristram might live at his court in safety and be always where he might see Isolde. But he did not keep his promise. He was always false and treacherous, and one day as Tristram sat at Isolde's feet, singing a song to her upon his harp, the cruel king came behind the knight and stabbed him in the back, so that he fell dead before his lady's eyes.

And that is the tragic ending of the sad story of Sir Tristram—the sorrowful born child.

THE MADNESS OF LANCELOT

SIR TRISTRAM was not the only knight of Arthur's court whose life was filled with sadness. Sir Lancelot, too, suffered much unhappiness because of the great love he bore for Guinevere, the king's wife. Arthur was a great king, good and just and kind, but he was not a great lover as Lancelot was. To Arthur, the excitement of the chase and the prowess of his knights and the honour and glory of the battle ranked far above his love for his wife. And so, perhaps, it is no wonder that in time Guinevere grew to love the brave knight, who served her with such devotion and performed such mighty deeds of arms for her sake, better than she loved the king who was her husband.

She loved Arthur still, she always loved him a little. And so did Lancelot, and for the sake of the king who trusted and loved them both, the two did their best to subdue the passionate love that they felt for each other.

THE MADNESS OF LANCELOT

But of all the things that are in the world, love is the greatest and strongest. And when men and women love truly, in the way that Lancelot and Guinevere loved, nothing can subdue it. They may perhaps be able sometimes to avoid any outward expression of it, but in their hearts it will be ever burning and glowing—burning all the more fiercely because they are obliged to hide it from other eyes.

Lancelot was the chief of the Knights of the Round Table, and the one to whom the king turned most often for advice. And except when he was riding upon some dangerous quest, he and Guinevere were forced to see one another almost daily. And because the two lovers were only mortal after all, and the strain of having to hide their love was sometimes almost too great for them, their tempers were tried to the breaking point. And one day the queen and her knight had a terrible quarrel. Guinevere was angry with Lancelot, and she said some bitter words to him, and Lancelot was so hurt and distressed at what she said that it affected his mind. He fell down to the floor in a swoon, and when he recovered he snatched up his sword and leapt out of the window and ran into the woods, not knowing what he was doing. For his great love for the queen had driven him mad.

THE MADNESS OF LANCELOT

When Guinevere heard what had happened she, too, was almost beside herself with grief, for she knew that it was her unkind words that had driven Lancelot mad. And she sent for three knights who were kinsmen to Lancelot, Sir Bors and Sir Ector de Maris and Sir Lionel, and begged them to ride in search of Lancelot and bring him back to her.

So Sir Bors and Sir Ector de Maris and Sir Lionel rode out in search of the mad knight. But though they searched for many a long day they could hear no news of Lancelot, and they grew more and more anxious and unhappy about him. At last they met another knight, who was on his way to Camelot. And they sent a message by him to the king saying that they could find no trace of Lancelot.

When Arthur received the message he was very grieved and sorry, and he called upon the other knights of the Round Table to go in search of their lost comrade. He had no lack of volunteers. Sir Gawaine and Sir Uwaine and Sir Perceval and many others at once started up and offered to go, and Arthur chose twenty-three of those who had offered, and sent them out to look for Lancelot in all parts of the country. But though they spent many weary months in looking, and met with many great adventures, they did not find the great knight.

THE MADNESS OF LANCELOT

Meanwhile Lancelot was living in the deep woods. He was so mad that he did not even know his own name, and he could remember nothing about his past life. He wandered about almost naked, wearing no more than a shirt, and he lived upon berries and wild fruits, and drank nothing but water from the little streams he found. He grew thin and gaunt and haggard, and roamed about from place to place—a man without a mind.

So for two years he ran wild in the forests; and then one day he wandered out into a meadow where a pavilion was set up. Close by the pavilion there was a tree upon which was hung a shield and two swords, while two spears lay below it. When Lancelot caught sight of the swords some little remembrance of his bygone knightly deeds came into his clouded mind. And he seized one of them in his hand and struck wildly at the shield, inflicting many grievous dints upon its fair surface.

The noise aroused those within the tent, and a tall knight with a dwarf attendant appeared in the entrance. The dwarf rushed at Lancelot and tried to pull the sword out of his hand. But Lancelot lifted him up in his arms and dashed him on to the ground, so that the dwarf cried out in pain and terror. Then the knight saw that it was a madman with whom he had to deal, and he said gently:

'Good man, lay that sword down. Methinks you stand more in need of food and clothes than you do of swords.'

But Lancelot answered him fiercely:

'Come not nigh me or I will slay you!'

The knight stepped back into the tent and called to the dwarf to come and help him put on his armour. Then, when he was fully armed, he approached Lancelot again, thinking to wrest the sword from him by force. But Lancelot sprang at him and smote him such a blow on the head with the flat of the blade that, even though the knight was wearing his helm, he was stunned and fell headlong to the ground. The sword broke into pieces with the force of the stroke, and flinging away the remnants of it, Lancelot rushed into the tent and flung himself upon the bed on which the knight had been resting when he was so rudely disturbed, and dropped off to sleep.

The knight, who had only been stunned for the moment, soon rose to his feet, and when he saw Lancelot lying asleep on his bed he was filled with pity for the noble-looking man who had come to such a sad state. And he determined to take him to his own castle, and see if he might not be cured of his madness. So while Lancelot slept men came and lifted up the bed on which he lay, and carried him, bed and all, into the castle of the kindly knight, whose name was Sir Bliant. Then they bound his hands and feet so that he might do himself no harm nor hurt any one else; and when he woke up they gave him good clothes to wear and the best of things to eat and drink. They soon brought him to health and strength again, but nothing that they could do could cure his madness or bring back his memory of things that were gone.

Then for many months Lancelot lived in Sir Bliant's castle, treated with the greatest kindness by the good knight and his lady, and by all around him. Except that his hands and feet were fettered he might have been an honoured guest, instead of a poor unknown madman whom they had found in a wood.

It happened one day that Sir Bliant was riding alone in the forest, when two cruel and wicked knights attacked him unawares. Sir Bliant did his best to defend himself, but the two knights together were too strong for him, and at last he turned his horse and rode fast towards his castle. The two knights rode hard after him, aiming blows at him as he fled, and for a little while Sir Bliant was in terrible danger. But Lancelot happened to be leaning out of one of the windows of the castle, and he saw the knight come riding towards the castle gate. When he saw what grievous wounds he was enduring he was filled with anger. In fierce indignation he broke the fetters from his hands and feet and rushed to help Sir Bliant, and, all unarmed though he was, he fell upon the two knights. With his bare hands he pulled one of them from his horse and wrested the sword out of his hand, and then he turned upon the other and gave him such a blow with the sword that he too was unhorsed. Then Sir Bliant, encouraged by this unexpected assistance, came to Lancelot's help, and the two knights fled away into the wood.

After that Lancelot's feet and hands were left unbound, and he was treated with even greater kindness than before. But though he had his freedom now and might wander where he willed, still his reason did not come back to him.

One day while the mad knight was wandering in the forest close to Sir Bliant's castle, a number of knights came riding past, chasing a huge boar. One of the knights alighted from his horse near to the place where Lancelot stood watching, and leaning his spear against a tree, sat down to rest. When Lancelot saw this, a fierce desire which he did not understand came upon him, and he longed to feel himself once more astride a horse's back. And before the astonished knight could utter a word of protest, he had seized the spear and sprung upon the horse and galloped off after the chase.

So fast did he ride that he soon outdistanced the other hunters, and at last he overtook the boar. The savage creature turned to bay against the side of a little hermitage, and when Lancelot rode at him with the spear he attacked the knight's horse and killed it. Nothing daunted, Lancelot continued the fight on foot, and although the boar gave him a dreadful wound in his side, it only served to madden him still further, and, exerting all his strength, he slew the boar.

The hermit had come out of his hermitage when he heard the noise of the fight, and he cried aloud when he saw the great gash in Lancelot's side that the boar's tusk had made. He would have taken Lancelot into his shelter and dressed the wound, but Lancelot in his madness did not know friend from foe. He turned upon the good man so fiercely that the hermit turned and fled. Lancelot tried to follow him, but he was so weak with loss of blood that he fell fainting upon the ground.

Then the hermit found some men to carry the wounded man into his hermitage, and there he nursed Lancelot until the wound was healed. But still the great knight was not cured of his madness, and as soon as he was well he went back to his wandering life in the forest again.

For another long while he lived amongst woods and lonely country places; but one day he came by chance to a city and passed through the streets. The boys and young men of the city laughed and jeered at the sight of a man dressed in such ragged garments, for the good clothes that Sir Bliant had given him had worn out by now. They threw stones at him and wounded him badly, but Lancelot turned upon them savagely and drove them away. But still, as fast as he drove some off, others gathered round him, throwing stones and clods of earth and even pieces of iron and other hurtful implements, until at last the noise they made aroused the attention of the knights who lived in a castle that stood in the midst of the town. When they saw the boys and young men tormenting a poor madman they were very angry, and they came down out of the castle and rescued Lancelot out of their hands.

They were all astonished to see such a noble-looking man in such a pitiable condition, and they said amongst themselves that he must surely be some great knight who had lost his wits. Even in his madness all could see that Lancelot was no ordinary man. And they gave him clothes and meat and drink, and took him to a little outhouse that stood in the castle grounds, where he might live and be at peace.

Now this castle belonged to a king named Pelles, who had one only daughter named Elaine. Elaine had often been to Arthur's court, and she knew Lancelot well by sight. She knew, too, the whole sad story of his madness, and one day, when she was in the garden, she saw the man whom her father's knights had rescued lying asleep beside a well, and she recognised him for the great knight of the Round Table—Sir Lancelot of the Lake.

She ran at once to her father and told him of her discovery. And King Pelles commanded that Lancelot should be lifted up while he slept and carried into a little room in the castle which the king and all his people regarded as a holy place. King Pelles was a descendant of Joseph of Arimathea, he who had taken Christ's body from the Cross after the Crucifixion. The story went that St. Joseph had stood by the Cross while the Roman soldier thrust a spear into the Saviour's side to make sure that He was really dead, and when he saw the drops of blood flowing from the wound had caught them in a cup as they fell. This cup, which was called the San Grael, or Holy Grail, had been brought by St. Joseph to England, so the legend ran, and sometimes in this little room a wonderful vision of it appeared. And the good king hoped that perhaps in this holy place the poor, mad knight might find healing for his mind.

And his hopes were fulfilled. That night, as Lancelot lay sleeping, those that watched him saw a mystic light in the little chamber, and they knew that the San Grael had come to heal the knight.

And when Lancelot awoke from his sleep his madness had passed away. He was as whole in mind and body as he had ever been.

But when he had heard the story of his madness he was ashamed to return to Arthur's court. So King Pelles gave him one of his castles to live in, and sent many of his knights to wait upon him, so that Lancelot might stay there for a little while until men should have forgotten some of the wild things he did when his madness was upon him. This castle was called the Joyous Isle, because it stood upon an island in the middle of a lake, and here Lancelot lived for a time. He would not call himself by his own name, for he did not want any one to know who he really was. So he called himself the Chevalier Mal Fet, which means the ' Knight who has Sinned.'

But although the knights and ladies from King Pelles' court who came with him lived in the castle in much merriment and happiness, it was anything but a Joyous Isle to Lancelot. Now that his madness had gone he remembered his lady again. His love for Guinevere grew ever greater and greater, and often he would steal away alone and weep with longing for her again.

One day, not far away from the Joyous Isle, a tournament was held, and news of it was brought to Lancelot. When the knight heard of it, all his old love for brave deeds and adventures rose up within him, and he sent messengers to proclaim aloud at the tournament that he was ready to joust with any knight who would come to his castle and do battle with him, and he promised that if any knight could overthrow him he might choose the best falcon he had in his falconry. Many brave knights came forward eagerly to joust against this strange knight of whom no one seemed to have heard before, but none of them succeeded in

Tristram carried his love away.

Page 99

Queen Guinevere loved the brave knight Lancelot.

Page 101

winning Lancelot's prize. No less than five hundred came to do battle with him, but, one after one, the great knight overthrew them all.

At last two of the knights from Arthur's court, Sir Ector de Maris and Sir Perceval, who had been searching through the world for many long years trying to find Lancelot and who had now almost given up their quest, came to the Joyous Isle. They were always eager for adventures, and when they heard of the Chevalier's challenge they sent to know if he would do battle with them. Lancelot was ready to try his skill against any who came, and he sent a gracious message to the two knights, bidding them welcome to his castle and asking them to come in. Sir Perceval was the first to encounter him, and for some time the two opponents fought with each other, neither seeming to gain any advantage. But in the end Sir Perceval was overthrown, and surprised at the skill of his adversary, the fallen knight cried out:

'I pray you tell me your name? Never before have I met with such a knight!'

'My name is Le Chevalier Mal Fet,' answered Lancelot. 'I pray you tell me yours.'

'I am Perceval of the Round Table,' said the other, as he rose to his feet.

THE MADNESS OF LANCELOT

Then suddenly Lancelot flung away his sword and dropped upon his knees.

'Alas! Alas! What have I done to fight against a knight of the Round Table?' he cried. And he told Perceval who he really was.

Sir Perceval was full of joy when he knew that Lancelot was found at last. He called for Sir Ector, and when Sir Ector came, Lancelot wept for joy to see his kinsman once more. The two knights told Lancelot how everybody at Arthur's court was mourning for him, and how sad Queen Guinevere was without her faithful knight. And when Lancelot heard of Guinevere's sorrow for him, his love for her broke down all his pride, and he felt that he could stay away from her no longer. And he rode back with his friends to Arthur's court.

Great was the joy at Arthur's court when Lancelot returned, for everybody loved the splendid knight. Arthur made great feasts in his honour, and nothing but rejoicings were heard on every side. Queen Guinevere wept for gladness when she saw him again, and her heart grew happier than it had been for many a long day.

So for a little while the lovers were together, and all misunderstandings were cleared away.

SIR GALAHAD

ONE day, not long after Lancelot had returned to Arthur's court, there came to Camelot a lady riding upon a horse, who begged that Sir Lancelot of the Lake might come with her, as she had something for him to do.

Lancelot asked what it was, but the lady would not tell him.

'You shall know when you have come,' she said. And Lancelot, who never refused a lady's request if he might grant it without dishonour to his knighthood or slight to the queen, called at once for his squire and told him to saddle his horse without delay.

Arthur and Guinevere were very disappointed that Lancelot should think of leaving them again so soon after his return, more especially as the next day was the Feast of Pentecost—a feast which was always celebrated with great rejoicings at the court. Guinevere ventured to plead with the knight as he stood waiting to depart.

'Will you leave us at this high feast?' she said wistfully, but the lady who had come for Lancelot answered for him.

'Madam, I will not keep him long. He shall be with you again by midday to-morrow,' she said. And with this assurance, Guinevere was obliged to let him go.

So Lancelot rode away with the lady, wondering what it was that she wanted him to do. They had not ridden very far when they came to an abbey, and the lady alighted at the door and took Lancelot inside. He was taken to a chamber, and then the abbess and her nuns came to him, bringing with them a fair boy of some sixteen years old.

'Sir,' said the abbess, 'we bring you here this child whom we have brought up in this abbey, and pray you to make him knight. For of all men in the world, you are the most worthy to give him the order of knighthood.'

Lancelot looked at the boy, marvelling at the beauty of his face and the grace of his form. Never had he seen such loveliness and purity of feature in a boy before.

'What is your name, and of what lineage are you come?' he asked. And the boy replied:

'My name is Galahad, and my grandfather is

King Pelles, and I desire greatly that you should make me knight.'

When Lancelot heard that he was the grandson of the king who had shown him such kindness in the terrible time of his madness, he was the more pleased to grant the boy's request.

'To-morrow, then, at the hour of prime, I will dub you knight,' he said.

All that night Galahad kept vigil in the chapel of the abbey; and very early in the morning, when the sun had just risen, Lancelot made him knight.

'God make you as good as you are beautiful,' the older knight said as the boy knelt before him. And his prayer was granted. For of all the knights of the Round Table there was never one who was as good and gallant and noble and pure of heart as was Sir Galahad.

When the little ceremony was over, Lancelot wished to take the boy back with him to Camelot. But Galahad shook his head.

'I may not come with you yet,' he said. 'Later on I will follow you.'

So Lancelot said good-bye to him and rode back to keep his promise to Guinevere.

He reached Camelot just before midday. The king and queen had just returned from the service at the cathedral. Arthur would have gone at once to the feast, but Kay, his seneschal, stood before him and reminded him that this was the Day of Pentecost, the day when he had decreed that he would never sit down to meat until he had heard or seen of some strange thing.

'If you go now to your meat, you will break your custom which you have kept all these years,' said Sir Kay.

'I had forgotten,' said Arthur. 'In my joy at having my brave knight, Sir Lancelot, with me again, I had forgotten the vow that I made.'

But the king did not have to wait long for his feast. Almost directly Sir Kay had spoken, a squire came in haste into the hall crying out :

'I bring unto you marvellous tidings, oh Sir King ! '

'What are the tidings you bring ? ' asked Arthur eagerly. And the squire answered :

'A great stone has come floating down the river and has stopped close to the shore below the castle. And in the stone there is a sword thrust fast. It is some great miracle and betideth wondrous things ! '

Then the king and all his court hurried down to the river's brink to see this strange thing. There, floating in the water as though it had been wood instead of stone, was a great block of red marble, into which was thrust a sword, the hilt of which was encrusted with precious jewels. Upon the sword was written in letters of gold :

'Never shall man take me hence but he by whose side I ought to hang, and he shall be the best knight of the world.'

When the king had read these letters he turned to Lancelot.

'This sword should be yours,' he said. 'You are the best knight of the world.'

But Lancelot shook his head sadly.

'No, Sire, that is not my sword,' he said soberly. 'I know full well that it shall never hang by my side. I will not even put out my hand to take it, for I know that I am not worthy to touch it.'

The king turned from him a little disappointedly, and said to Gawaine :

'Will *you* try the adventure of the sword ?' And Gawaine, who was always willing enough to undertake any adventure, put out his hand and grasped the sword boldly and endeavoured to pull it from the stone. But the sword would not yield to his pulling, nor to that of any of the knights who were bold enough to try.

SIR GALAHAD

At last Sir Kay turned away from the river.

'Now you may go to your dinner with a good conscience,' he said to the king. 'For you have in truth seen a marvellous thing to-day.'

So the king and his knights went in to dinner and sat down in their places at the Round Table. Just as they were served an old man came into the hall, leading by the hand a young knight, who proved to be none other than the boy whom Lancelot had knighted that very morning, Sir Galahad.

'I bring you here a new knight, who comes of king's lineage, to be one of your knights of the Round Table,' said the old man.

'Sir, he is welcome,' said Arthur courteously.

Now at the Round Table there was one seat in which no man had ever sat. When the table had first been brought to Arthur's court, Merlin had warned the king never to let anybody sit in it.

'It is to be kept for one who will come to claim it in due time,' the wise man had said. 'If any man be so hardy as to sit in this seat until the rightful owner comes, death and disaster shall surely overtake him.' And the knights had been very careful to obey Merlin's commandment. The seat had been kept covered with a cloth ever since, and it was always known as the 'Siege Perilous,' or the Perilous Seat.

But now to everybody's amazement the old man led Galahad to this very place, and taking the cover from it he bade the boy sit down. And Galahad did as he was told, for on the seat was written in letters of gold :

'This is the seat of Galahad.'

Then the old man went away and left Galahad at the court, and the feast went on.

When dinner was over the king called his new knight to him and spoke to him kindly, and told him of some of the wonderful things that had happened at the court. And amongst other things he told him of the strange stone that had floated down the river, and how none of the knights might move the sword.

Then Galahad answered quietly :

'Sir, that is no marvel, for the sword is mine. Here by my side hangs the scabbard, but I brought no sword with me, for it was told me I should find my sword at Camelot.'

Then the king took Galahad down to the river, and all the knights and ladies followed them to see if it were indeed true that the sword belonged to Galahad. And Galahad put out his hand and grasped the hilt of the sword and drew it out of the stone and put it into his scabbard.

'Now that I have my sword I am ready for the adventures that shall come to me,' he said.

The king and his courtiers were amazed that this boy should have been able to draw the sword when so many strong knights had tried and failed. The king remembered that once he had been able to do almost the same thing, and he knew that it was a miracle wrought to show that this boy knight was destined for some great quest. And all the other knights treated Galahad with awe and reverence, remembering the writing on the sword.

THE QUEST OF THE HOLY GRAIL

ON the evening of the day upon which Galahad came to Camelot, the king and his knights were sitting at supper at the Round Table. They were talking of all the wonderful things that had happened during the day, when suddenly there came a thunderclap which shook the castle to its foundations, so that the knights thought that the walls were falling upon them. But before any of them could move from their places, a brilliant ray of light shone through the castle hall, brighter by far than the brightness of the noonday sun. And down the ray came gliding a vision—a cup covered by a gleaming white cloth—and the knights knew that it was the Holy Grail itself.

So dazzling was the light, that none of them could have seen the holy cup clearly, even had it not been veiled with the cloth. And as they sat in silent awe and wonder, holding their very breaths in their amazement, the vision disappeared. The mystic light departed, and the knights drew breath again and began to speak in low tones of the wonder they had seen.

Then another wonderful thing happened. On every knight's plate was found the meat he liked the best, set there by unseen hands while the Grail passed through the hall. The king and his knights were filled with still more awe and astonishment, and some of them began to fear a little, feeling that they were on holy ground.

But Gawaine, who was always ready to rush into any adventure, rose to his feet and, with never a thought as to whether he were worthy to undertake so high a quest, cried out :

'We have been served with meat and drink such we love the best, but could any one of us see clearly the Holy Grail ? It was so closely covered, I scarce might distinguish its shape beneath the cloth. Wherefore I make a vow that to-morrow I will ride out in quest of the holy cup and strive if I may not see it without the veil.'

When the other knights heard Gawaine's rash vow, they too sprang to their feet and swore that they also would ride out in quest of the Holy Grail. King Arthur was grieved and displeased when he heard the vows they made, for he knew that few of them, if any, were worthy to accomplish the quest. And yet, now that they had sworn they must endeavour to fulfil their vows, although there was little hope of their being able to do so. For none might gaze upon the holy cup in all its unveiled splendour, unless he were perfectly true and pure in mind and soul and body. And gallant and brave though the knights of the Round Table might be, yet they were but men after all, and could hardly hope to lay claim to such perfection as this.

'Alas!' said Arthur. 'I am bereft of the truest knighthood and the fairest fellowship that ever was seen in this world. For I am sure that many of you who ride upon this quest shall never return to Camelot again. The beginning of the end of the Round Table is come.'

The tears came into many eyes at the king's sorrowful speech, and some of the knights began to regret their hasty vows. But it was too late to draw back now. The queen and all her ladies wept openly when they heard the news, and the night was passed by all in sorrow and mourning. When day came, the king and all who had vowed to ride upon the quest went to the Cathedral, to hear mass and to dedicate themselves afresh to God before starting upon their journey. Then many sad good-byes were said, and the knights mounted their horses and rode through the streets of Camelot while the people crowded round them, bidding them farewell. King Arthur accompanied them to the gates of the city, then he turned away and went sorrowfully back to his court.

So this goodly company of knights rode out into the world to seek the full vision of the Holy Grail. But Arthur had been right in his foreboding. Of all the hundred and fifty brave men who set out upon the quest, only four of them ever saw so much as a passing glimpse of the holy cup, and only *one* of those four ever saw it in all its unveiled beauty. And many of those who rode through the gates of Camelot that summer morning, never, by summer or winter, rode back through them again.

Sir Lancelot, who was one of the company, soon parted from the rest of his companions. He had no definite plan in his head, and he rode in whatever direction seemed best to him at the moment. For some time his path led him through a great forest, but after awhile the forest ended, and he found himself in a dreary waste of country. It was beginning to grow dark, and when presently he caught sight of a little chapel in the distance, he rode towards it, hoping to find people there who would give him shelter for the night.

But when he reached the chapel he found that it was all ruined and broken down, while there were no signs of human habitation anywhere around. Still Lancelot determined to seek shelter within the ruined walls, and alighting from his horse he tied it to a tree while he went on foot to explore the little chapel.

When he came to the building he was surprised to see within it an altar covered with a fair white cloth, on which stood a silver candlestick with six branches, bearing six tall candles all burning and alight. Then Lancelot attempted to enter the chapel, but to his great astonishment he could not pass through the open door. Some invisible force seemed to stand in his way and hold him back, so that at last he was afraid to try again. Then he went back to his horse and unharnessed it so that it might rest, and putting his shield upon the ground he lay down upon it and fell asleep.

As he slept he saw a wonderful vision. It seemed to him that two white horses came by, bearing a litter upon which lay a sick knight, who moaned and wept and cried aloud :

'Oh, God, when may I be saved from this sickness by the holy vessel which I seek ?'

Then Lancelot saw a little table set up beside the

litter by invisible hands, and the silver candlestick floated out from the ruined chapel and stood upon the table. And then suddenly the holy cup itself, the Holy Grail in quest of which the knights of the Round Table were riding, appeared upon the table also. The sick knight's face lighted up with joy as he saw it, and he crawled from his litter and knelt before the table and took the cup in his hands and drank deep from it. And as he did so his sickness left him and he was made perfectly whole.

Then the table and the candlestick and the holy cup disappeared, and all was dusk again.

All this Lancelot saw in his sleep, but though he tried to move and wake himself up, some spell seemed laid upon him so that he might not stir hand or foot. The knight who had been healed came and stood over him and looked down upon him, and while he so stood a squire came to him, bringing with him arms and armour. The two men remained for a few moments gazing down at Lancelot, and in his dream Lancelot heard the knight say :

' This is some knight of the Round Table who has entered into the quest of the Holy Grail. Yet is he not worthy to look upon it save in his sleep.'

Then he took the armour his squire was carrying and dressed himself in it. And it seemed to Lancelot that he took the shield upon which he himself was lying from under him, and mounted Lancelot's horse and rode away.

Then at last Lancelot awoke. He thought at first that it was all a dream that he had dreamed. But as he lay, half-waking and half-sleeping, he heard a voice above him say :

'Sir Lancelot, go from hence, for thou art not yet worthy to stay in this holy place.'

Then Lancelot roused himself fully, and he found that his shield and his horse and his sword had all gone, and he feared greatly, knowing that he had seen a vision in his sleep. He went away from the place on foot, very sorrowful of heart.

'I see now that I was not worthy to take upon me this adventure of holy things,' he said to himself.

For the rest of that night and for the most part of the next day, too, he wandered on on foot, until at last he reached a hill at the foot of which stood a little hermitage where a hermit was saying mass. Lancelot stayed while mass was said, weeping and sobbing, and after the service was over the hermit came to him to ask if there was anything that he could do. Then the knight told the old man of the high quest he had undertaken and the vision he had seen the night before, and how he feared that he was not worthy to have ridden forth upon such a holy adventure.

'For all my great deeds of arms that I have done, I did them not for God's sake, but for the queen's, that I might be better beloved. And always have I done battle for her, whether it were right or wrong, not for any worship or praise of God,' he said.

When the hermit had heard all the story, he placed his hands on the knight's bowed head, and told him to take comfort.

'For you are a good man and a brave knight, and God will surely have mercy upon you if you turn to Him,' he said. 'But, nevertheless, you shall never see the full beauty of His holy cup, for it is ordained that none but the pure in heart may see the vision with their mortal eyes. Yet despair not, for much shall be granted you, and you shall do penance for your past sins and be made clean and whole again. And if you will but love God as well as you have loved your queen, He will surely have forgiveness for you and pardon all that you have done amiss.'

Then the hermit gave Lancelot a hair shirt that he might wear it always, and so remind himself to bear arms for God's honour and glory for the future and not only for love of the queen. And he gave him also a horse and a shield and a sword to take the place of those the knight had lost. Then Lancelot, after he had thanked the good old man for his help and counsel, rode once more upon his way, and after that he did not forget to pray to God always that he might be counted worthy to achieve the quest.

He passed through many dangers and encountered many wonderful adventures, and overcame difficulties that might have daunted lesser men. But still he went boldly forward, until at last after many months of lonely wanderings he came at midnight beneath a castle's walls. The door into the castle was open, and two lions lay guarding it, and as he reached it Lancelot heard a voice saying :

'If thou have courage to enter the castle, thou shalt see a great part of thy desire.'

Then the knight drew his sword and went towards the door, prepared to do battle with the lions that lay in the path. But suddenly his sword was smitten out of his hand, and the voice said again :

'Oh, man of little faith ! Shall not He in whose service thou are set, avail thee more than thine arms ! '

Lancelot was ashamed of his mistrust, and picking

up his sword he put it into his sheath and walked on unarmed towards the door. And the two lions drew back to let him through, so that he entered into the castle without hurt. As he went along he found that every gate and doorway was open so that he might pass by without let or hindrance.

But at last he came to a room the door of which was shut fast, so that he could not open it. A sound of sweet singing came from within the room, singing more sweet than any that had ever been heard on earth. And Lancelot knew that within the room was the holy cup he had come so far to see.

Then he knelt down and prayed earnestly to God to grant him just one vision of the precious vessel; and as he prayed the door was opened and a wonderful light shone upon him, and Lancelot sprang to his feet and would have entered the room, but a warning voice said:

'Nay, Lancelot, enter not the room.' And the knight drew back and bowed his head, sad to think that he might not come nearer to the Holy Grail.

After awhile he lifted his head once more and looked into the chamber. He saw there an altar surrounded by a fair company of angels, holding candles and palms in their hands, while upon the altar stood the holy cup itself, covered with a red cloth. A priest stood before the altar, and as Lancelot watched, the holy man took the cup, still covered with the cloth, in his hands and lifted it towards heaven. And it seemed to Lancelot's wondering eyes that the cup changed into the figure of a man—the Saviour Himself. The knight thought he saw the priest stagger a little beneath the weight which he upheld, and fearing lest he should drop his precious burden, Lancelot sprang forward into the chamber, forgetting the warning he had received.

Then suddenly a fire came between the rash knight and the altar, and Lancelot was flung backwards upon the ground, and lost all power of seeing or moving or hearing. He felt himself lifted by invisible hands and borne out of the room and laid upon the ground outside the chamber door. And then a great darkness fell upon him and he lay as one dead.

For four and twenty days he lay there as in a trance, knowing that he was alive, but unable to speak, or to move hand or foot, or to open his eyes. But on the twenty-fifth day he awoke from his swoon, and rising reverently he went away, thanking

God for having brought him safe through his adventure and for having granted him at last a vision of the Holy Grail. For though even yet he had not looked upon the holy cup unveiled, yet he had seen more than was vouchsafed to most mortal men. And he knew that he should never see the vision clearly while he was in his earthly body.

So he rode back to Camelot, the first of the knights of the Round Table to return from the quest.

HOW GALAHAD ACHIEVED THE QUEST

THE boy knight, Sir Galahad, was one of the gallant company that rode out upon the quest of the Holy Grail. When he left Camelot he was still without a shield, but in spite of his lack of full armour the young knight had no fear. He had been told that both sword and shield would be given to him in due course : the sword had already been provided, and he knew that the shield would come to him also when the proper time came.

For four days he rode on without meeting with any adventures. On the evening of the fourth day he came to an abbey where two other knights were staying. Galahad decided to spend the night there with them, since it was growing so late.

Now at this abbey there was kept a wonderful silver shield, marked in the centre with a red cross, which was said to bring death or disaster to any man who bore it, unless that man should be the best knight in the world. The monks had guarded it carefully until its rightful owner should come to claim it, but though many knights had attempted to carry the shield away, as yet none had been found who was worthy to bear it. Before he had ridden many miles each knight who had borne it had met with death or some terrible wound.

One of the knights who was spending the night at the abbey declared during supper that he was going to try and take the shield for his own. The monks warned him against touching it, but the knight would not heed their words.

'I know well that I am not the best knight in the world,' he said. 'Nevertheless, I will attempt the adventure. And if I be slain, as you tell me, then must Sir Galahad claim it.'

And the next morning he took the shield down from behind the altar where the monks had hung it, and turning to the young knight, he said :

'Abide here at the abbey until you see how I shall speed.' And calling to his squire to follow him, he rode away.

But the adventurous knight was not allowed to ride far with the magic shield. He had only gone a very little way when a strange knight came riding towards him. This knight was dressed all in shining white armour, and he rode upon the other knight and bore him from his saddle.

HOW GALAHAD ACHIEVED THE QUEST

'None save he who is the best knight in the world may bear this shield,' said the White Knight sternly, as he stood over his fallen opponent. Then he turned to the squire who was standing trembling in the background.

'Bear this shield back to the abbey whence it came, and give it to the good knight, Sir Galahad,' he commanded. And the squire, not daring to disobey him, rode back at once to the abbey.

When the monks heard the squire's tale, they knew that Galahad was the knight for whom they had been keeping the shield. They blessed the young man and watched him set forth upon his great quest, and then they themselves went to carry home the man who had so rashly tried to take away the shield, and who was lying sorely wounded upon the ground in the place where he had encountered the White Knight. The good men took him back to the abbey and did all that they could for him, and in the end the knight recovered, though for a long time he was in great peril of death.

But Galahad, armed with his sword and shield, rode out in quest of the Holy Grail. He, too, did not ride far before he met the stranger knight. But this time the White Knight made no attempt to take away the shield. He drew rein when he reached Galahad's side, and saluted the young knight courteously.

Galahad returned the salute, and when he had thanked the White Knight for sending him the shield, he ventured to ask him from whence it came. The knight told him that it had once belonged to an English king who had lived in the days of Joseph of Arimathea, when the great saint had brought his precious relic from the Holy Land.

'At one time this shield had no cross upon it,' the White Knight told Galahad. 'But when St. Joseph lay dying, the king, who had loved and followed him in many of his wanderings, begged that he would leave him a token by which he might remember him. St. Joseph told him to bring him his shield, and when the sorrowing king brought it to the dying man's side, the saint traced from his own blood a cross upon its fair surface. And this same shield has been kept for you, Galahad, because it is ordained that you shall achieve the quest of the Holy Grail.'

Then the White Knight vanished from sight.

The young knight thanked God for giving him this wonderful shield, and then he rode on with renewed courage, determined to fight bravely against all sin and wickedness until at last he should be accounted worthy to accomplish the quest.

And many great and wonderful deeds did Sir Galahad perform. So brave and valiant was the young knight that none could stand against him. Everywhere he went he fought against tyranny and wickedness, righted wrongs, overthrew cruel men who hurt and oppressed helpless people, succoured ladies in distress and set poor captives free, so that his name became famous throughout the world. But never once did Galahad forget the high mission upon which he was bound. Never once did he fall into sin or yield to any grievous temptation. He kept himself pure in heart and soul and body, for he knew that it was through purity alone that he could ever hope to achieve the vision that he sought.

One night Galahad took refuge with a hermit, who, when he knew that his visitor was a knight-errant, was only too glad to entertain him. When Galahad had eaten and drunk the two lay down upon the floor of the hermitage to rest, but they had not lain there long when there came a great knocking at the door. The hermit rose up to see who was there, and when he had opened the door he saw a young girl standing outside, holding a palfrey by the bridle.

' Sir, I would speak with the knight who is with you,' the maiden said, and the hermit went back and told Galahad that he was wanted. When Galahad came to the door, the girl said :

' Arm yourself, Galahad, and come with me, for I am sent to help you upon your great adventure.'

Galahad knew at once that the maiden had been sent to him by God, and he went back and took his arms and mounted upon his horse and rode after the lady. The maiden spoke not a word until they came to the seashore where a little ship was waiting for them. Then she turned to the knight and said :

' We will leave our horses here, for this ship shall bear you to the land where you shall achieve the quest of the San Grael.'

Galahad dismounted from his horse and turned it free, and then followed his guide on board the ship, where, to his great joy he found two other knights of the Round Table, Sir Bors and Sir Perceval, both of whom were bound upon the same quest as himself. When the three knights had greeted each other, Galahad asked them where the ship had come from, but neither Sir Bors nor Sir Perceval could tell him that. It had come to Perceval as he knelt upon the seashore, thanking God for having delivered him from a great danger.

He had entered into it and it sailed with him over the sea, until of its own accord it came to shore again, where Sir Bors had joined him. And then it had sailed on once more.

When Perceval had finished his story, the maiden turned to him.

'Do you not know who I am?' she said. And when Perceval had looked at her long he recognised her as his sister whom he had not seen for many years. There was great joy then on board the little ship, and the three young knights and the maiden had much pleasant talking together about the high adventure upon which they were bound, while the vessel sailed on of its own accord, seeming to know exactly the way it had to go.

When day dawned the next morning, the voyagers found that the ship had brought them once more close to land. A castle was in sight, built close by the sea, and as they had no food with them the little party landed, meaning to ask the people who lived in the castle to give them some. But as they approached the gates an armed knight rode out to meet them.

'You shall not depart hence until this maid has yielded to the custom of the castle,' cried the knight; and as he spoke many other knights ran out and surrounded the travellers, while several ladies came hurrying after them. One of the ladies held a silver bowl in her hands, and the knight of the castle told the indignant young men that no maiden might pass by that way unless she gave enough blood from her right arm to fill the bowl.

The three young knights were very angry when they heard of this cruel custom, and Galahad cried :

' You shall not touch this maiden while I live ! '

Perceval and Bors both said the same, and they set upon the knight of the castle and his attendants and drove them back through the gates. But no sooner had they driven back the first party than other knights came forth to do battle with them, and yet other knights, so that the three from Arthur's court could take no rest at all.

But when night fell at last, the knight who had first accosted them called for a truce. And he invited the knights of the Round Table to come into the castle and rest.

' As we be true knights we will do you no harm,' he said. ' For this one night we will be friends, although on the morrow we must fight again unless this maiden will accord us the custom of the castle.'

So the three young knights and the maiden went into the castle, and the knight treated them with every courtesy and set before them all that they could desire. Then Galahad asked why such brave and gallant men as the knights of the castle seemed to be, should maintain a custom which was contrary to all the laws of chivalrous knighthood.

Then the knight told them a sad story. The castle, he said, belonged to a lady who had been ill for many, many years. She was suffering from a very terrible sickness, and it had been prophesied that she would never be made any better until she had been anointed with the blood of a maid who was as pure in heart and mind as she was in body. But though many maidens had given their blood to try and heal the mistress of the castle, none of them was pure enough, and the lady still lay in terrible pain and anguish at death's door. Then her faithful knights, who loved her dearly, had sworn a vow that no maiden should pass the castle gates until she had yielded a bowl full of her blood —in this way they hoped that one day they might find a cure for their lady's sickness.

'And so we may not let you pass until this damsel has given us of her blood, else shall we be forsworn,' said the knight.

Perceval's sister had been listening entranced to this strange story, and now her heart was filled with pity for the poor lady who suffered such dreadful pain. And she begged her three companions to let her give her blood without further battle, and see if she might not avail to save the lady's life. The three young knights were very reluctant to consent to her wish, but the maid would not take 'No' for an answer. She declared her intention of doing as the custom of the castle demanded, whether they would let her or not.

'But if you lose so much blood, you may die yourself,' said Galahad, but the girl answered:

'What matters it if I do, since I die to heal another. I shall but win for me great worship and soul's health. And perchance if I be found as pure in heart and mind as I am in body, the lady may be healed, and then this wicked custom shall no more prevail.' And she told her companions that, even though they died fighting to save her, still she would yield to the custom.

So in the end they were obliged to let the brave girl have her way. The sick lady was brought forth, and the girl's pure blood was taken from her arm and carried to the invalid's side, and when she had been anointed with it the lady of the castle was healed from her sickness. But she was only saved at the cost of the brave maiden's life, for Sir

HOW GALAHAD ACHIEVED THE QUEST

Perceval's sister grew so weak from loss of blood that she fell fainting upon the ground. And though her brother and his friends did all they could for her, they could not save her from death.

She smiled up at her brother as she lay dying.

'Fair brother, grieve not for me,' she said. 'It was ordained that this should be, and when all things shall be known, you will find that this is no cause for sorrow. But now, I pray you, as soon as I be dead, lay my body in a boat and let me go forth as the winds shall lead me. And when you three have come to the city where you shall achieve the quest of the San Grael, there shall you find me waiting for you. Bury me in that city, and you and Galahad also shall be buried in the same place.'

Perceval wept bitterly as he promised to grant her request. Then the brave maiden died, and the three knights carried her body to a barge and laid it reverently down, covering it with a pall of black silk. No sooner had they done this than a great wind arose which blew the little boat until it was out of sight of land. Then, with weeping and mourning, the three knights turned away.

They did not at once go back to the ship which was to bear them to the end of their adventures. They were warned by a voice that they must depart from one another until their deeds should make them more worthy still to accomplish their quest. So the next morning the three friends separated, and each rode on his way through the world, seeking adventures in strange places, endeavouring by every means in his power to fit himself for the great achievement. For nearly two years the three rode on their lonely ways, but at last one day they met each other again, and then indeed their joy was great. For they knew that it was God who had brought them together, and that now they would not be parted again until the quest was fulfilled.

As they rode side by side, telling each other of all the adventures that had befallen them since they had last been together, they came to the castle where King Pelles lived, he who was Galahad's grandfather and had shown such kindness to Lancelot in the time of the great knight's madness. They were very glad indeed when they found where they were, for they knew that in this castle the vision of the Holy Grail had been sometimes seen, and they hoped that perhaps some passing glimpse of it might be shown to them also.

Their hopes were not disappointed. King Pelles was overjoyed to see his grandson, and he made a feast for him and his two friends. And as the knights sat round the table, a great light shone around them, and a voice said :

'Let all those depart save they who are upon the quest of the San Grael.'

Then King Pelles and his knights rose from the table and passed out of the room, leaving only the three young knights from Arthur's court in the room. As these three sat waiting for what might happen next, a great number of armed knights, who seemed scarce mortal men but visitants from some other world, came into the chamber and, laying aside their arms and helms, sat down in the empty places round the board. After they had taken their seats, four women came into the room, bearing a stretcher upon which lay a sick man with a crown of gold upon his head. The women set the stretcher upon the ground close to Sir Galahad, then they disappeared, and the sick man raised himself painfully upon his bed and spoke to the young knight.

'Galahad, I have waited long for your coming,' he said. 'Three hundred years have I lain here in pain, waiting until the purest knight in all the world should come to set me free. But now the time has come when my pain shall be allayed, and I shall pass out of the world to find the joy and happiness that has been promised me. I am that king to whom St. Joseph of Arimathea gave the shield that you now bear. And I have been kept alive all these years until your coming, that the glory of the Lord might be revealed.'

Galahad gazed with awe and wonder at the holy man who had lived for such a long, long time. And his heart was filled with joy to think that he should have been chosen to perform such wonderful deeds. And then a wonderful vision was seen in the room. It seemed to Galahad and his two companions that their Lord Himself came to them and showed them the wounds He had received upon the Cross, and fed them Himself from His holy cup. And He blessed them, and told them that now they might go and find their ship again, and it should bear them to the city where they should achieve the quest.

Then the vision vanished, leaving the three knights filled with holy joy. For though they had not yet gazed upon the cup in its unveiled beauty, yet they knew that they had been nearer to doing so than they had ever been before in all their lives.

When they had come to themselves again, they saw lying upon the table before them a spear which seemed to be shedding drops of blood. They knew it for the spear with which Christ's body had been pierced by the Roman soldier as He hung upon the Cross; and taking it reverently in his hands Galahad bore it to the king who had been waiting for his coming for so many years. No sooner had the spear been laid upon his body, than in a moment the king was healed of his long sickness. He started to his feet, praising and thanking God for having given him back his strength; and after Galahad and his friends had departed again upon their quest, he went to an abbey to spend the rest of the time that remained to him on earth amongst the holy monks.

It was midnight when that wonderful supper came to an end, and at once Galahad and the other two knights took their armour and hastened to obey the directions that had been given them. They rode hard for three days, and then they came to the sea, where to their joy they found the ship in which they had sailed before waiting for them. They entered at once, and in the ship they found a little silver table, standing upon which was a cup covered with a red cloth. They knew it for the Holy Grail from which they had been fed a few days before, and they knelt down before it in prayer and reverence. But they did not touch it, or try to lift the cloth in which it was wrapped. For they knew that they must wait for God Himself to show it to them in His own good time.

The ship, guided by some unseen power, bore them quickly away from the shore, and sailed on until at last it came into the harbour of a foreign town. As the three knights landed and drew their ship to shore, they saw a black barge coming to land also, and they recognised it as the barge in which they had set Sir Perceval's sister adrift so many years before. The maiden's body lay there still, just as they had laid it down.

'Well hath my sister kept her promise to us,' said Perceval. And they took her body up out of the barge and buried her in a manner befitting the daughter of a king.

Then they went back to their own ship and brought away from it the silver table and the precious cup covered with the red cloth. The table was heavy and they staggered a little under its weight, and Galahad called to a beggar who was sitting at the gate of the city and asked him to come and help them bear the table.

The old beggar man looked at him in astonishment. He was so bent and old and crippled that there was some reason for him to be surprised.

'Lo, these ten years have I been a cripple and

may not move save that I go upon crutches. How can I help you bear the table?' he said. But Galahad answered him encouragingly.

'Nevertheless, arise up and show your good will to help,' he urged.

The crippled man rose to his feet, and came hobbling upon his crutches to the young knight's side. And no sooner had he touched the table than the strength came back into his limbs, and he was as sound and well as ever he was in all his life. Then he cast away his crutches, and helped to bear his share of the table's weight, crying aloud to all who were near to see how he was made whole.

The people of the city flocked together to see the knights who had wrought this marvellous cure. But the king of the city was a cruel and wicked man, and when he heard of the wonderful powers possessed by the strangers, he was afraid lest his people should turn away from him and follow the three knights. And he sent his soldiers, and took Galahad and Bors and Perceval prisoners and shut them up in a deep dungeon, where he did his best to starve them to death. But though the wicked king gave his captives no food or drink for a whole year yet they did not die. For every day the Holy Grail came to them and gave them food and drink.

But even yet they never saw the holy cup uncovered. Always it was veiled from their eyes.

After they had been for a year in their dreary prison, the king of the city fell ill. He was dying, and, when he knew that he could not recover, his heart repented of the cruel way in which he had treated his prisoners. When he heard that the three men were still alive, he sent for them out of their dungeon and begged them to forgive him for all that he had done. The three knights gave him their full forgiveness, and then the king died.

After the king was dead, his people came together in counsel wondering whom they should choose to reign over them. As they were debating amongst themselves, a voice cried aloud in their midst :

‘ Choose ye the youngest of the stranger knights to be your king.’

Galahad was the youngest, and he was made king in the presence of all the people, who were glad indeed to have such a noble man to be their ruler. He ruled the city wisely and well, and the people soon grew to love him, and never regretted their choice. Galahad’s first care was to see to the safety of the Holy Grail. He made a little chapel in his palace, and set the silver table in the sanctuary. Then he placed the holy cup upon the table, and built a cover of gold and precious stones to go over it.

For a year Galahad ruled over the city, while Sir Bors and Sir Perceval gave him their assistance and advice. When the anniversary of the day upon which he had been crowned came round, the three knights rose up very early in the morning and went into the palace chapel to pray. But when they reached the chapel they saw a man, dressed in the robes of a bishop, standing before the altar, celebrating mass, while all around him stood a great company of angels. The chapel was filled with a dazzling light, and the three knights sank upon their knees, while Bors and Perceval hid their faces in their hands.

The man at the altar called to the young king:

'Galahad, thou servant of Christ, come now and thou shalt see clearly that which thou hast so long desired. I am Joseph of Arimathea, and I am come to show you the full vision of the San Grael.'

Then Galahad came near to the altar, and he lifted up his eyes, and for the first time he saw the full vision of the Grail. The cup shone out before him in all its unveiled loveliness, and he looked upon it with eyes that might at last see it in all its beauty. And he cried out with a loud voice:

'O Lord, I thank thee for granting my desire! Fain would I be at rest and live no more, for now at last have I achieved my quest.'

The cup still shone before him, and in obedience to a gesture from the holy man, he knelt down and received the sacrament. And when he had received it, the angels bore his soul away.

When Sir Bors and Sir Perceval were at last able to lift their eyes to the altar, the vision had vanished. Gone was St. Joseph, gone was the great company of angels, gone was the dazzling light, and gone too was the holy cup. Galahad was still kneeling before the altar, but, when his two companions went to him, they found that he was dead.

After that Perceval and Bors went to live in a little hermitage outside the city, for Perceval knew that he had not long to live, and he wished to end his days in holiness. Sir Bors stayed with him until he died. Then he buried him beside his sister and Galahad, and after that he himself took ship and sailed over the sea and came to the court of King Arthur, and told the king and his knights of the ending of the quest of the Holy Grail.

And after the death of Sir Galahad, the Holy Grail was no more seen by any mortal eyes.

QUEEN GUINEVERE AND THE POISONED APPLES

WHEN the quest of the Holy Grail was ended, those knights who were still alive came back to Arthur's court, and the king tried to form again his great company of the Round Table. But Camelot was never again to know the glory of the days that had been. Many of the knights who had ridden forth upon the quest never returned, and those who did come back had grown sad and changed, as though they knew that the end of Arthur's glorious reign was drawing near.

Sir Lancelot was one of the most changed of all the knights. He still loved the queen with passionate devotion, but he no longer showed his love for her in the way that he used to do, and the queen was sometimes hurt by the change in him. She, too, still loved the knight as much as ever, but she did not understand Lancelot quite in the way that she had been used to understand him, and she often wept and reproached him with having lost his love for her. And at last Lancelot, unable to endure her reproaches any longer, went away from the court, and only Sir Bors, his kinsman, knew what had become of him.

Guinevere was very unhappy when Lancelot had gone, and she longed to have him back again. But she was too proud to show her sorrow outwardly, and in order to hide from other people how deeply she was suffering, she tried to bury her grief in pleasure. And she made a great feast and invited all the knights of the Round Table to come to it, and all who could do so accepted her invitation.

Now Sir Gawaine was very fond of all kinds of fruits, and, knowing this, Guinevere had set a dish of apples on the table especially for him. But one of the knights had a grudge against Gawaine, and unknown to anybody else he had poisoned these apples, thinking that Gawaine would be certain to eat them. His plan, however, went astray, for another knight, named Sir Patrise, took one of the poisoned fruits and ate it, and to everybody's horror he fell down dead.

All the knights started to their feet in dismay, and Sir Mador, who was cousin to the dead knight, was filled with grief and anger. Everybody suspected Guinevere of having tried to poison Sir Gawaine, and though the queen protested her innocence, nobody believed her. The king was sent for in haste, and Sir Mador openly accused the queen of having murdered his cousin and demanded that justice should be done.

Arthur was filled with dismay when he heard what had happened. Although he had no such love for the queen as Lancelot had, yet in his way he loved his wife, and he did not for one moment believe that she was really guilty of having killed Sir Patrise. But he was king, and he felt that it was his duty to see that justice was done. He determined to give Guinevere a fair trial, and if she was then proved guilty, he made up his mind that, queen though she was, she must suffer the pain of death by burning, as though she had been any other poor lady.

'I command you to be present in the meadow beside Westminster, fifteen days from now,' he said to Sir Mador. 'Then, if any knight come forward to do battle for my queen, you shall fight together, and God shall speed the right. And if no knight come forward to battle, or if the queen be proved guilty, she shall be burnt to death upon that day in the sight of all people.'

'I will be there,' said Sir Mador, and then the company broke up and the knights went away.

But they all believed the queen to be guilty, and no man would come forward to do battle for her. Arthur was in despair, for if no knight at all came forward, Guinevere would be adjudged guilty and would be given to the stake without any trial at all.

'Where is your knight, Sir Lancelot?' he demanded of the queen. 'If he were here, he would surely fight for you?' And he reproached the queen for having quarrelled with her faithful knight and driven him from her side.

Poor Guinevere wept bitterly, and longed for her lover to come and deliver her from the cruel death that lay before her. She knew not where Lancelot was, and no other knight came forward to be her champion, and for many days it seemed that she would have to die without any trial at all. But at last Sir Bors, Lancelot's kinsman, came forward and offered to do battle for her, and the queen was glad to accept him as her champion, although she knew that it was only for love of Sir Lancelot and not because he thought her innocent that Bors had come.

All too soon the day came when the queen's trial was to take place. A great pile of faggots was built upon the field about an iron stake, in order that the queen might receive her punishment at once if Sir Mador should overthrow her champion. Guinevere herself was brought out to witness the fight, and the king and all his courtiers came to the field to see what would happen.

It was a terrible time for Guinevere. But she held her head high and would not show her fear and sorrow, although she had good cause to dread the outcome of the battle. For although Sir Bors was a good and brave knight, yet he was not very skilful at deeds of arms, and she scarcely dared to hope that he would overthrow her accuser.

When the judges had taken their seats, Sir Mador rode out and took his oath before the king.

'I swear,' he cried, 'that it was the queen who did this treason to my cousin, Sir Patrise. And here will I prove it with my hand and body to all who say the contrary.'

Then Sir Bors, as the queen's champion, rode out and took his stand beside him.

'And I,' he said, 'swear that Queen Guinevere is innocent of this crime, and with my hands will I declare that she is not guilty.'

'Prove your vows upon your bodies, then,' said Arthur. 'And God defend the right!'

But before Sir Bors and Sir Mador could meet in battle, a strange knight, dressed in unknown armour, came riding quickly upon the field.

'Fair knight, this is my quarrel,' he said to Sir Bors. 'I pray you withdraw, that I may do battle for the queen.'

Then, raising his voice so that all might hear, the knight cried :

'I am come here to fight for Queen Guinevere against all her accusers. She is innocent of this foul charge that hath been laid to her, as I will here prove. Therefore, Sir Mador, guard yourself, and God shall show which of us twain hath right.'

Then he rode at Sir Mador and battled with him so fiercely that the queen's accuser was overthrown and obliged to yield himself to Guinevere's champion in order to save his life.

'Declare Queen Guinevere innocent of all treason, or die,' said the stranger, as he stood with drawn sword above his fallen foe.

And Sir Mador cried out :

'She is innocent. Hereby I discharge my quarrel against her for ever.'

Then the strange knight put back his sword into its sheath and threw back his helm so that all the people might see that it was Sir Lancelot of the

Lake who had come to the queen's rescue. Sir Bors, knowing his own weakness and the queen's great danger, had sent to tell the knight of the trial that was to take place, and Lancelot had come just in time to save his lady from the fate that awaited her.

A great shout went up from the people when they recognised him, and Lancelot went to where the queen was standing before the stake and took her by the hand and led her to the king. And Arthur came down the steps of his dais to meet his wife, and he kissed her tenderly in front of all the people, and thanked Lancelot again and again for having rescued her.

'Nay, my lord king, there is no need to thank me,' said Lancelot. 'Right glad am I to have been of service to my queen, for, as you know well, I am sworn to be her knight, and her knight only, so long as my life shall last.'

Guinevere's pride, which had sustained her all through her terrible ordeal, had quite broken down now. She wept bitterly as she added her thanks to Arthur's, and she reproached herself more than ever for having said such unkind things to Lancelot. Then all the other knights came crowding round to welcome Lancelot back, and to ask pardon of the queen for having so misjudged her. And while they were all gathered together, the mysterious Lady of the Lake, who had been Arthur's guide and helper upon so many occasions, suddenly made her appearance in their midst.

'The queen is innocent of the death of Sir Patrise,' said the Lady of the Lake. 'It was Sir Pinel le Savage who did the evil deed and upon whom Sir Mador should have taken vengeance. But now he is escaped out of the land.'

The knights were still more ashamed of their evil suspicions when they heard these words, and Guinevere's name was cleared from any thought of wrong. Sir Mador was overcome with sorrow and remorse and knew not how to atone to the queen for his unjust accusations. But Lancelot interceded for him, and Guinevere was so happy to have her knight back again, that she was only too glad to grant his request and accord Sir Mador her full forgiveness.

And so for a little while things were made right between the lovers again.

THE MAID OF ASTOLAT

NOT very long after Lancelot had delivered Queen Guinevere from death, Arthur called his knights together to take part in a great tournament which was to be held at Winchester. Knights and nobles from all parts of the country gathered to this tournament, and a few days before it began, the king and his knights of the Round Table left Camelot to ride to the field where the fighting was to be held.

Sir Lancelot did not ride forth with the king and the rest of the knights. He stayed behind at Camelot for a little while, pleading as an excuse that he was not yet quite whole of a wound Sir Mador had inflicted upon him on the day when he fought for the queen. But it was only an excuse. As soon as Arthur had gone, he too took his horse and armour to ride to Winchester, for he quite meant to take part in the tournament. Only he meant to fight in disguise so that no man might know him. Men had been saying of late that knights went down before him in battle because of the fame of his great achievements, not merely because they were inferior to him in strength, and Lancelot was determined to prove whether this was really so, or whether it was because he still retained his wonderful skill in deeds of arms.

On the evening before the tournament was to take place, Lancelot came to the castle of Astolat which was within a few miles' ride of the field appointed for the fight. The knight dismounted from his horse and knocked at the gates of the castle and asked if he might take shelter there for the night. The lord of the castle welcomed him gladly, although he did not know who his visitor was, and took him to the best chamber where Lancelot laid aside his armour and put his weapons down.

'I would that you would lend me a shield that is blank,' said the knight, as his host assisted him to disarm himself. 'To-morrow I ride to joust at this tournament, and I have a mind to carry a blank shield that no man may know who I am.'

'Fair sir, I will lend you one right willingly,' answered the Lord of Astolat. 'I have two sons that were but lately made knights, and the elder was hurt the same day that he was knighted, and may not yet ride out to battle. His brother,

Lavaine, is all afire to ride to the jousts to-morrow, and if you will take him with you as your squire, you shall have his brother's shield that bears as yet no sign or mark upon it, in place of your own. But, I pray you, will you not tell me your name, that I may know who it is that lodges with me ?'

'Nay, sir, I beg that you will hold me excused from telling you that,' said Lancelot. 'If I come back safe from the lists, then will I surely tell you. But until the battle is over I would fain keep my name secret from all the world.'

The lord of the castle did not press his guest to tell him who he was, but took him down to his hall and entertained him courteously. Besides his two sons, the old baron had one only daughter, a lovely young girl just reaching womanhood, whose name was Elaine. Elaine had never before seen any knight who was so brave and courtly and handsome as Lancelot, and as he sat and talked with her father and her two brothers, her heart went out to him, and she fell in love with him.

Lancelot was very kind to the little girl—for she seemed no more than a little girl to him. He talked to her and told her wonderful stories of Arthur's court and his own great adventures, little dreaming of the great love for him that was springing up in the maiden's heart. And when presently Elaine asked him shyly if he would wear a token of hers at the tournament the next day, he consented with a smile, saying:

'I have never worn a token for any woman before. But if you will show me yours, mayhap I will wear it, if you will so honour me.'

He did not know what importance Elaine would attach to his consent, or he would never have granted the shy request. He thought to himself that he could hardly have a better disguise than to wear a maiden's token. For all Arthur's knights knew that he would never wear a woman's favour when he jousted—if he wished to fight unknown he could not find a better way of hiding his identity.

But poor little Elaine thought that since the great knight had consented to wear her token that he must surely have fallen in love with her, as she had fallen in love with him. And she ran joyfully to fetch her token, a red sleeve embroidered with pearls, and Lancelot bound it upon his helm, saying that it would surely bring him good success. Then he gave the maiden his own shield to keep for him until he should come to claim it again, and smiled once more at the enthusiasm with which the girl undertook the charge.

The next morning the knight rode away to the tournament, bearing on his arm the blank shield which the Lord of Astolat had lent him, and taking with him the younger of the baron's two sons, the young man Lavaine, who had fallen almost as much in love with the great knight as had his little sister Elaine.

They came at length to the field where the tournament was to be held, and there Lancelot threw in his lot with the weaker side. Young Lavaine followed him into the battle, and both of them won great honour and renown. Everywhere that Lancelot went his opponents fell down before him, until all men marvelled who the stranger could be who did such mighty deeds of arms. None of them recognised him for Sir Lancelot because of the red sleeve he wore upon his helm. Even his own kinsmen did not know him, and they became very jealous that Lancelot's deeds should be outshone by this stranger.

'Oh that Lancelot were here to-day that he might uphold the honour of his name,' they said. And they rode furiously at the unknown knight and came upon him altogether and bore him from his horse, while one of them, Sir Bors, who loved Lancelot better perhaps than any of the knights at Arthur's court and would have died himself sooner than hurt him if he had only known, wounded him grievously in the side with his spear.

Lavaine saw his companion fall, and he rode quickly to his help. He fought back the knights who were gathered around him, so that the wounded knight managed to struggle into his saddle again. Then he and Lancelot fought side by side, and Lancelot, in spite of his wound, dealt such valiant strokes around him that in the end the other knights were driven back. Then the heralds blew their trumpets and proclaimed aloud that the prize was won by the unknown knight who wore the red sleeve, who had done more gallantly than any knight that had ever fought upon the field.

But Lancelot was too hurt to stay and receive his prize. He turned his horse and rode quickly from the field, while Lavaine in great concern rode after him.

Lancelot managed to keep his seat until they came to a little wood and were out of sight of the field of battle. Then he slid from his horse's back and waited for Lavaine to reach him.

'Help me pull this spearhead from my side,' he gasped. And Lavaine saw that the head of the spear with which Sir Bors had wounded him was still in the knight's side. The younger knight managed to pull it out, but the blood flowed from the wound in such quantity that Lancelot fell fainting upon the ground. Lavaine was in deep distress, and seeing an hermitage not far away he rode and called to the hermit to come and help him. The hermit came at once, and he and Lavaine carried the wounded knight into shelter and removed his armour and tried to dress the wound.

The hermit had once been a knight of the Round Table himself, who had left his great deeds and rich possessions to live a holy life for God. When he saw Lancelot he recognised him at once.

' It is Lancelot of the Lake,' he said, and Lavaine, although he had not known for certain who his companion was, was not surprised. For after the wonderful deeds he had seen the knight perform that day, he had guessed that he could be none other than the great Sir Lancelot himself.

When King Arthur and his knights saw the knight who had fought so bravely ride wounded from the field, they were very sorry. And Gawaine, who had applauded the stranger's brave deeds loudly, sprang to his feet and called for his horse.

' By my head ! ' he cried. ' If that knight may be found at all, I am going to find him, for he is the very best knight that I ever saw, and pity is it indeed that he is so sorely hurt!' And followed by his squire, he rode off the field and endeavoured to overtake Lancelot and Lavaine.

But he missed the little wood in which Lancelot had taken refuge, and though he rode all around the countryside for many days, inquiring everywhere he went for a wounded knight who wore a red sleeve in his helm, he could find no trace of the man for whom he sought. At last, discouraged, he turned back to Camelot, but, since it was growing late, he decided to ask for shelter at a castle that he could see in the distance.

It was the castle of Astolat, and when the baron heard that his visitor was Sir Gawaine, a knight of the Round Table, he welcomed him joyfully and begged for news of the tournament. Gawaine told them of the fight and how a strange knight wearing a red sleeve in his helm had won the prize, and as he spoke, Elaine, who was listening to his tale, clapped her hands with delight.

'God be praised that he has sped so well!' she cried.

'Why, do you know him then?' asked Gawaine. And the baron told him how the knight had come to spend the night with them, and how they had given him a blank shield to bear in place of his own since he wished to ride disguised to the tournament.

'We know not his name, for he would not tell it us,' put in Elaine. 'But he gave his shield to me that I might take care of it until he should come again to claim it. And I have covered it with a silken covering, and keep it safely in my chamber until he comes.'

'Let me see it,' said Gawaine, beginning to suspect who this strange knight might be. And when the shield was brought and the silken covering was taken from it, he recognised it at once.

'It is Lancelot of the Lake,' he said. 'And now am I sadder than ever I was before. For the knight was sorely wounded, so sorely that I fear that he must die. And if Sir Lancelot dies the greatest glory of Arthur's court will be departed.'

Then Gawaine rode back to Camelot, bearing with him the sad news that the stranger who had been so hurt in the tournament was none other than Lancelot. But Elaine, the maid of Astolat, begged her father to let her go in search of the wounded knight that she might nurse him back to health. The old baron gave his permission, for he loved his daughter dearly and never denied her anything that she asked. And the girl rode away from her home and searched the country round, and never rested until at last she came to the little hermitage where Sir Lancelot lay.

There, by day and night, she nursed the man whom she had learned to love so well, until at last Lancelot recovered of his grievous wound and grew well and strong again. Then Elaine and her brother brought him back to their father's castle, where the Lord of Astolat and his elder son received them with great joy.

Elaine was very happy for a little while, but at last the time came when Lancelot must depart, All this long while the girl had been expecting the knight to ask her to marry him, and she could not understand why he did not do so. She had lived so out of the world that she did not know that Lancelot had given all his love to the queen and could never love any other woman. And at last, when the time came to say good-bye to the knight, she felt that she could not let him go, and, overcoming her shyness and maidenly reserve, she told him all that was in her heart and begged him to marry her.

When Lancelot heard her request he was filled with dismay. He loved his girl companion, it is true, but only in the way he might have loved a child, and he never dreamt that Elaine had cared for him like this. He could not bear to distress and hurt the poor little girl, but all the love he had to give was given to Guinevere long years ago, and he knew that it would be wrong for him to marry Elaine when he bore in his heart this great unchanging love for another woman, even if he could have brought himself to do so. As gently as he could he refused the girl's petition, though it went to his heart to grieve her so. Elaine fell fainting to the ground with shame and sorrow when Lancelot told her that he could never do as she required, and the great knight stood by in deep distress as he watched her women carrying her away.

The next morning he rose up very early and left the castle of Astolat, for he felt that he could no longer remain with the good old baron upon whom he had brought such sorrow. Lavaine went with him, for the young knight loved and worshipped Lancelot as much as his sister did, though in a different way. He could not bear to be separated from his hero, and determined to follow him wherever he went so long as they both should live.

But poor Elaine might not follow the man she loved so dearly. She had to stay behind in the castle, feeling that all the sunshine and happiness had gone out of her life for ever. But she did not live very long to mourn her lost knight. She had always been fragile and delicate, and now her unhappiness affected her health so greatly that a deadly sickness laid its hold upon her. Her grief-stricken father did all that he could for her, but she grew ever weaker and weaker, until at last she died.

Just before she died she sent for her father and her elder brother and begged them to write a letter for her to Lancelot. She told them what to say, and then she begged them to promise her that when she was dead they would dress her in her richest robes and lay her in a barge with the letter in her hand, and send the barge down the river to Camelot. Her father, who was broken down with sorrow at the thought of losing his only daughter, gave his promise that all should be done as she wished; and when the girl was dead, he and his son carried out her wishes faithfully.

They dressed her in her richest robes and laid her in a barge which they draped with black hangings. They put the letter she had made them write in her hand, and laid a coverlet of gold over her body, and then they sent the barge down the river in charge of an old dumb serving-man.

THE MAID OF ASTOLAT

Meanwhile Lancelot had reached Arthur's court again, where the king and his knights received him joyfully. But Guinevere had heard the story that Sir Gawaine had brought back with him after he had seen Lancelot's shield in the care of Elaine—how Lancelot had fallen in love at last with a girl who was little more than a child, the fair and only daughter of the Lord of Astolat. And, because Lancelot had worn the red sleeve at the tournament as a favour, a thing he had never done before, the queen thought that Gawaine's gossiping tale must be true. She was dreadfully hurt and angry with her knight, and when he came back to court she would not speak to him, or give him the least chance to explain how it was he had come to wear the red sleeve. Lancelot tried many times to see her and explain and make things right again, but always the queen evaded him, until at last he, too, grew hurt and angry at her continual distrust, and so once more these two lovers were sorely estranged.

They were both very unhappy at their estrangement, and the time passed away very slowly and sadly for them, and then at last, one day, there came floating down the river a barge covered with black draperies upon which lay the body of a beautiful maiden, dressed in the richest and most costly robes. The barge was steered by an old, old man, who spoke no word in answer to any inquiry, and when it drew level with the castle grounds the dumb servitor brought it to shore, and made it fast to the landing-place. The news of the strange arrival spread quickly through the castle, and all the lords and ladies came flocking down to the water's edge to see the wondrous sight. The king and queen came too, and when Arthur saw the letter clasped in the maiden's hand, he took it gently from her and opened it and read it aloud.

It was a sad little letter, and the reading of it brought tears into the eyes of the men and women who listened. It was addressed to 'The Most Noble Knight, Sir Lancelot,' and it prayed him that since he could not love the Maid of Astolat, he would at least make supplication for her soul. Arthur sent for Lancelot and the maid's brother Lavaine, and when Lancelot came and had heard the letter and saw Elaine lying so fair and beautiful, her sweet face shining like a star against the black of the barge, the tears came into his eyes, too, with pity for the child who had died for love of him. Then he told the king the story of how he had spent the night before the great tournament at the castle of Astolat, and how, thinking the maiden to be but

Galahad saw a castle, built close by the sea.

Page 141

At last Elaine came to the little hermitage where Lancelot lay.

Page 172

a child, and never dreaming of the great love she bore him, he had consented to wear her favour at the lists. And then he went on to tell how Elaine had nursed him back to health when he was so sorely wounded, and how she had begged him to marry her, and how shocked and grieved he had been when he had learned what her real feelings for him were, and how he had been obliged to ride away at once without staying to bid her good-bye.

And Lavaine, as he knelt weeping beside the dead body of his sister, bore witness that the knight's words were true.

Then the queen was ashamed of her suspicions, and she sent for Lancelot and told him how sorry she was that she had wronged him with her doubts.

'Ah, madam, this is not the first time you have been angry with me causelessly,' said Lancelot with a sigh, and the words moved Guinevere to even greater remorse.

'Lancelot, forgive me!' she said, holding out her hands to him. And Lancelot forgave her, for he loved her too much to be angry with her for long.

Elaine was buried at Camelot with great reverence and pomp, and her sad story was written upon her tomb. Lancelot and the queen both mourned for her for many days, for though they had been made friends again and were happy in each other's love, they were sorry and ashamed to think that it had needed the death of this sweet, tender-hearted child to bring them together.

HOW GUINEVERE WENT A-MAYING

ONCE more winter passed away, and once more springtime came round at Camelot. And when the month of May came again, and the weather grew warm and sunny, Queen Guinevere felt a longing in her heart to ride out into the green woods and fields, and see the world growing young and fresh again.

So, accompanied by her ladies and by a few of her faithful knights, she rode forth early one morning into the woods and meadows to enjoy the fresh spring air. The sunlight daneed about them, the daisies and buttercups sprang up beneath their horses' feet, and the may-flowers were white upon every hedge and thicket. The queen had given orders that all those who rode a-maying with her should come dressed in green robes to be in keeping with the springtime of the year. And so the knights laid aside their armour and took only their swords with them, for none of them dreamed that danger could befall upon this happy expedition.

But there was a knight who lived in a castle not

very far away, who had loved the queen for many years and longed to have her for his own. He had watched for a chance to steal her from Arthur for a long time, but always Guinevere, when she rode abroad, was surrounded by knights and men in armour, and usually Sir Lancelot of the Lake rode by her side. And this knight, whose name was Sir Meliagrance, was too afraid of Lancelot and his companions to dare to attempt to carry off the queen whenever they were near.

When it was told him by his spies that Guinevere was going a-maying on the morrow, and that orders had been given that all who rode with her were to lay aside their armour and go clothed in green, his heart was filled with fierce joy, for he knew that his opportunity was come. He called together his men-at-arms and his archers, a hundred and twenty of them in all, and the next day, when the queen and her ladies and the ten knights who were accompanying her were maying in the woods, he came upon them in ambush and carried them away to his castle.

But when Guinevere saw that her knights were being overpowered by Meliagrance and his men, she took a ring from her finger and gave it to a boy page who was riding by her side.

'Ride swiftly to Sir Lancelot and give him this ring and tell him what has befallen,' she said in a low tone. 'And pray him, as he loves me, to come and save me from this wicked knight.'

The page-boy took the ring and, watching his opportunity, made good his escape. Sir Meliagrance saw him riding away, and he ordered his archers to shoot at him. But the arrows fell wide of their mark, and the boy was soon out of danger. He rode on at his utmost speed until he found Sir Lancelot, and then he gave him the ring and told him the story. Then Lancelot was consumed with fear for the queen's safety. He did not wait to summon any other knights, but, telling the page to carry the evil tidings to the king, he flung himself upon his horse and set off in hot haste to overtake Sir Meliagrance.

In such fear for the queen was he, that he did not stay to ford the rivers when he came to them, but plunged his horse in at the nearest places and forced him to swim across the waters. Very soon he came to the spot where Sir Meliagrance had set upon the queen; but the wicked knight, when he saw that the page had escaped, was in deadly fear lest Lancelot should come after him, and he had left a party of thirty archers concealed in the wood, with orders to shoot anybody who might come in pursuit. When the archers saw Lancelot riding so furiously towards them, they drew their bows and let their arrows fly. They shot Lancelot's horse dead beneath him, but their arrows glanced harmlessly off the knight himself, for he was clothed in full armour.

Sir Lancelot rushed at the archers with his spear, and the archers fled in haste, fearing his vengeance. Lancelot could not overtake them, for they were fleet of foot while he himself was cumbered with his heavy armour. He dared not take any of it off, for he feared the treachery of Sir Meliagrance, and he knew that he would need it all later on if he ever came face to face with his foe.

Just at this moment a cart came by driven by two men. They were some of Sir Meliagrance's servants, and they had come to fetch wood for their master. When Lancelot saw the cart, he commanded the men to stop and let him ride with them. But the men refused to do so, and, full of anger, Lancelot dealt one of them a blow that knocked him from the cart and stretched him dead on the ground.

The other man was terrified when he saw the fate of his companion, and he cried out to Lancelot :

' Sir Knight, do not slay me, and I will drive you where you will.'

'Then drive me quickly to the castle of Sir Meliagrance,' said Lancelot. And the man helped him into the cart, and lashed up his horses and set off at a great pace towards the castle of the treacherous knight.

As soon as they reached it, Lancelot sprang down from the cart and beat upon the gates until the whole castle rang with the noise that he made.

'Where art thou, false traitor?' he cried. 'Come forth—for here am I, Lancelot of the Lake, that shall do battle with you!' And he flung himself so furiously against the gates that they gave way before him; and he sprang through and killed at one blow the porter who tried to keep him back. Then he rushed madly through the courtyard, calling for Sir Meliagrance, while the terrified servants scattered left and right before him.

But when Sir Meliagrance heard Lancelot's angry voice, he was far too terrified to come out and do battle with him. He ran to the queen and flung himself upon his knees before her, and begged her to forgive him and to intercede for him with Lancelot.

'Tell him I have done you no harm! Tell him he shall have all in my castle to do with as he likes! Tell him that I will be his slave for evermore, if he will only spare my life!' he cried in anguish, as he grovelled piteously at her feet.

Guinevere could not help feeling sorry for the spectacle the craven knight made in his terror. She drew her robes contemptuously away from his shaking hands.

'You are not worth that any man should fight you,' she said with disdain. And she went down to where Lancelot was still thundering out his challenge in the courtyard below, and begged him to spare the life of Sir Meliagrance.

Lancelot was very unwilling to allow the treacherous Meliagrance to escape the punishment due to him. But he was too glad to find the queen safe and unhurt to refuse her her request. He consented to let the craven knight go free, and then all those who had been taken prisoner with Guinevere were set at liberty, and the queen and her company rode back to Camelot.

THE HEALING OF SIR URRE

AT the time when all these great adventures were taking place in England, there lived in a country far away across the sea a knight whose name was Sir Urre. He was very brave and gallant, and he travelled all over the world wherever he heard that any fighting might be found. And one day, in a tournament in Spain, he fought against a knight whose name was Sir Alphegus, and overthrew him and killed him.

He slew him in fair battle, but the mother of Sir Alphegus was full of anger for the death of her son, and she swore to be avenged upon the knight who had overthrown him. In the battle, Sir Urre had received seven wounds from his opponent's spear, and the mother of Alphegus, who was a sorceress, wrought an enchantment so that Sir Urre's wounds should never be made whole.

'They shall never heal, but shall bleed and fester for ever, unless they are touched by the best knight of the world,' she said when she had finished the enchantment. Not even with her wonderful powers could she contrive that they should be left unhealed without hope of any cure. But the hope she was obliged to leave was so far off and difficult of attainment, that she thought to herself in triumph that it was almost as good as though it had never existed.

The words of the angry Spanish lady were brought to the ears of Sir Urre's mother as she was grieving over her wounded son. And when she learnt that there was just one way in which Sir Urre might be healed, this brave woman made up her mind that she would search through the world until she had found the best knight in it. She caused a litter to be made upon which Sir Urre might be borne without too much discomfort, and then she and her daughter, taking with them one attendant to look after their horses, left their home and all the luxuries to which they had been accustomed, and set out with Sir Urre to look for the best knight of the world.

Through many countries the little party journeyed, and whenever they came to castles or palaces the lady begged the knights there to touch the wounds of her son to see if he might not be made whole. For seven long years they wandered, and Sir Urre's wounds were touched by many knights and kings and noblemen, but no help was to be found in any of them. It seemed as though they would never discover the best knight of the world.

But still Sir Urre's mother did not lose heart. She took ship at last and sailed over the seas, and so in course of time she came to England and reached King Arthur's court. When Arthur heard the story of her fruitless search, his heart was filled with pity for her and her son, and he commanded all his knights to come together and touch Sir Urre's wounds, to see if by any chance there might be one amongst them who could make the sick man whole.

'If Galahad were here, he should surely be healed,' the king said. 'But Galahad, alas! is dead long since, and I know not now if there be any knight in my court who is worthy to be called the best knight in the world. Nevertheless every man here shall lay his hands upon him, and I myself will touch him first to encourage other men to handle him after me.'

Then the king touched the wounds of the sick man in order that the rest of the knights should not be afraid to try if they held this healing power to cure the sick man. But though, one after another, every man present touched the body of Sir Urre, the knight's wounds could not be made whole.

But one knight of the Round Table was not

present at the gathering that day, and that was Sir Lancelot of the Lake.

'Where is Sir Lancelot?' asked Arthur when all the other knights had tried to heal Sir Urre and failed, and even as he spoke Lancelot came riding into the courtyard of the castle. He dismounted from his horse and saluted the king, and then Arthur told him the story of Sir Urre, and how he and all his knights had tried to heal him.

'You, also, must touch his wounds as we have done,' said the king.

But Lancelot hung back.

'Nay, my lord king, who am I that I should dare to call myself the best knight of the world,' he said. 'Where so many other knights and noblemen have failed, I cannot hope to succeed. I dare not take upon myself this task.'

'You have no choice in the matter, I command you to touch Sir Urre,' said Arthur. 'For so have I promised his lady mother, that every knight of my court shall try if he may not heal him.'

Then Sir Urre sat up feebly upon his litter and stretched out his hands towards Lancelot pleadingly.

'Most courteous knight, I pray you in God's name to touch my wounds and try if you may not heal me!' he begged. And Lancelot could not resist this piteous appeal.

'Would God I might help you,' he said. 'But I know I am not worthy to do so high a thing. Nevertheless, since my lord Arthur commands me, I must do his behest, though it is sore against my will.'

Then the great knight knelt down beside the sick man. And as humbly and simply as though he had been alone in his chamber, he lifted up his hands to God and said:

'I beseech Thee give me power to heal this sick man—not of myself, great Lord, but of Thine own mercy and virtue.'

Then, still kneeling, he touched the wounds of Sir Urre with reverent fingers. And as he touched them, by some miraculous power they were made whole, and Sir Urre rose from his litter, and for the first time for seven years stood upright on his feet.

When the king and the knights saw this miracle they fell upon their knees and gave praise and thanks to God with great rejoicings. But Lancelot bowed his face upon his hands and wept as though he had been a little child. He was glad indeed to think that God had given him power to heal the sick man, but he was not vain or proud because he had been proved thereby to be the best knight in the world. He knew himself how sinful and wicked he often was, and his tears were tears of penitence and sorrow.

To celebrate Sir Urre's recovery, Arthur made a tournament in which many of the knights of his court took part. Sir Lancelot and some of the older knights of the Round Table did not joust that day, but stood aside to let their younger fellows carry off the honours. Sir Urre took part in it, however, and so well and strong had he become that he overthrew all the knights who came against him and won the prize the king gave.

After that Sir Urre stayed always at Arthur's court and never returned to his own country. He had determined never to leave Lancelot, but to stay with him and serve him and wait upon him always. For he loved the great knight who had healed him better than any other person in the world.

THE PASSING OF ARTHUR

ALTHOUGH Arthur still held his court at Camelot, and many brave and glorious deeds were still performed by his knights, the wonders of his reign were nearly over, and the noble fellowship of the Round Table was drawing to an end. The quest of the Holy Grail had been, as the king had foreseen, the beginning of that end; and though some knights returned safe from the quest, and though other knights were elected to fill the places of those who did not come back, there was never the same loyalty and happy comradeship amongst them as there had been in the days before Sir Gawaine made his rash vow. Jealousies and quarrels cropped up, knights had disputes with one another which led to lifelong feuds, and in some cases open warfare was proclaimed.

Lancelot and Gawaine in especial had a terrible quarrel. Once when the knights were fighting together, Lancelot killed Sir Gareth, Gawaine's brother. It was quite by accident, for Lancelot loved Gareth dearly, and he was dreadfully grieved when he found what he had done. But Sir Gawaine never would forgive him. He had always been a little jealous of Lancelot, and a bitter quarrel began between the two knights which did not end until Gawaine was dead, and Arthur's kingdom was broken up and all the fellowship of the Round Table scattered abroad.

Gawaine appealed to King Arthur for help against Lancelot; and Arthur, who was growing jealous at last of the great love between Guinevere and his knight, threw in his lot with him and made war upon the Knight of the Lake. Lancelot left the court, and gathered his kinsmen and friends about him and made ready to defend himself against the king. It almost broke his heart to have to bear arms against his lord, for he loved Arthur, who had given him knighthood and who up to now had shown him nothing but courtesy and kindness. And he knew, too, that although the war was not of his seeking and he was blameless in many ways, yet he was not altogether innocent. He had loved the queen too well, and shown his love for her too openly.

'My fault lay in trying to serve the king when I bore such love to the queen,' he thought to himself.

But it was too late to undo any of his actions now, even if he would have had them undone. He could only abide the consequences. And the consequences were very terrible for Arthur and for all the knights. The war dragged on and on, and many brave men were slain on either side, until at last Lancelot and his followers took ships and sailed over the sea and took refuge in a castle in a foreign land.

But still Gawaine's anger would not be appeased. Although Lancelot was now banished from his own country, Gawaine urged the king to follow him and destroy him utterly. And Arthur listened to his knight's unwise counsel. He made a great army ready, and prepared to sail over the seas to besiege Sir Lancelot in his castle and make an end of him. Before he left the court he called his nephew, Sir Mordred, to him, and made him ruler over the kingdom while he should be away. Then he, and Gawaine and others of his most trusted knights, sailed over the sea to continue the war against Lancelot.

For many months Lancelot was besieged in his castle, and many more brave men were killed on either side. Every day Sir Gawaine stood before the castle gates and called upon Lancelot to come forth and fight him in single combat, but for a long while Lancelot would not heed the taunts and threats that he made. For he knew that he was stronger than Gawaine, and he could not bear the thought of fighting to the death against one who had once been his friend. But at last he could endure Gawaine's taunts no longer, and upon an appointed day he came forth from his castle, and the war ceased for awhile while all the warriors on both sides gathered to see the two knights do battle.

It was a long fight, for Gawaine was determined to kill Lancelot if he might, while Lancelot did not wish to do more than overthrow Sir Gawaine. For a long while the onlookers knew not which way the battle would go, but at length Lancelot dealt his adversary a blow that felled him to the ground. Then, as Gawaine lay on his side expecting the other knight to finish the battle and kill him, Lancelot put his sword into his sheath and walked away.

'Why withdrawest thou?' cried Sir Gawaine. 'Turn again, false traitor knight, and slay me, for I swear unto you if you leave me thus, so soon as I am whole I shall do battle with you again.'

'Be it so,' said Lancelot. 'I will abide you, but whatever may betide I will never slay a fallen knight.'

And in spite of Gawaine's mocking words and taunting threats he strode back towards his castle.

So the war went on, while Gawaine lay sick of his wounds, fretting and fuming to do battle with Lancelot again. It was a month before he was well enough to bear arms, and even then he was not able to issue another challenge to his foe. For such grave news came from England, that Arthur was forced to raise his siege of Lancelot's castle and hurry back to defend his realm.

Sir Mordred, his nephew, whom he had left in charge of his kingdom, had turned traitor to him. As soon as Arthur had gone, Mordred had plotted and planned to get the kingdom for his own. He had written letters which seemed as though they had come from over the sea, saying that Arthur was dead in battle. And he showed these to the chief of the nobles who were left in England, and made them believe that their king was dead. Then he had had himself crowned king, and had declared his intention of marrying Guinevere, his uncle's wife.

When he heard that Arthur knew of his treachery and was hurrying home to regain his crown, Mordred raised an army and marched to Dover to oppose the king's landing. But he might not stand against the fury of Arthur and his knights. His army was badly beaten and he was obliged to flee quickly away. But yet the battle was not without much loss and harm to Arthur. For Sir Gawaine, who for all his hot temper and revengeful nature was yet one of the loyalest and truest of all the king's followers, was wounded so sorely that he died soon after the battle.

Before he died Gawaine repented of his hot temper and hastiness.

'All this trouble has come upon you through me,' he said to the king. 'It has all come through my feud with Lancelot. Were Lancelot here, your enemies would not have dared to rise against you.' And he begged the king to send for Lancelot and forgive him and take him into favour again.

Then he died, and the king mourned and wept for him. But his tears were of no avail, and he was obliged to bury Sir Gawaine at Dover and then march against Mordred, who had gathered his beaten forces together and was preparing for another battle.

Again Mordred was beaten, but again he rallied his forces, and then once more a terrible battle was fought, the last battle he and Arthur and many other brave men were ever to fight. All day long the fighting raged, and there was terrible slaughter on both sides, until at last when darkness began to fall there were but four men left alive upon the field—Arthur and two of his knights, Sir Bedivere and Sir Lucan, who were brothers, and the traitor Mordred himself.

At last when all but these lay dead or dying, the king and his two knights ceased from fighting and gazed sadly around them. Arthur's heart was heavy within him as he looked at his fallen men, and when he saw Mordred standing alone amongst his own dead warriors, the king's wrath overflowed. He seized his spear in his hands and ran towards his nephew, crying out:

'Traitor! Now is thy death day come!'

Sir Mordred turned at the cry, and when he saw the king running upon him, he drew his sword and prepared himself to meet him. But Arthur's spear ran him through the body before he could escape the onslaught, and Mordred knew that his hour of death had come. He lifted his sword in both his hands, and smote Arthur upon the head with such force and strength that the sword pierced through the king's helm and sent him staggering to the ground. Then he himself fell down dead

Sir Lucan and Sir Bedivere hurried to the king's side and lifted him up in their arms. Not very far away there was a wide lake, and through the gathering gloom the two knights could see the ruins of a small chapel which stood close beside it. There would be a little shelter for the king there, they thought, and together they carried Arthur to it and laid him gently down upon the floor.

But Sir Lucan had been seriously wounded in the past battle, and the effort of lifting the king was too much for him. The blood gushed out of his wound and he swooned upon the ground and died. Bedivere wept bitterly when he saw that his brother was dead. But his tears could not bring Sir Lucan back to life, and so he turned again to the king to see if he could not recover him from the faint into which he had fallen.

Presently the king regained consciousness, but he also was too grievously wounded to live and he knew that his end had come. He raised himself feebly upon his elbow and gazed around him, and when he saw the lake lying below in the distance he suddenly remembered where he was. It was the very spot where the Lady of the Lake had given him his sword so long ago, and as he recognised it he recalled the words that she had spoken to him.

'When the time comes you shall give it back to

me again,' the Lady of the Lake had said, and Arthur knew that the time was come.

He turned to Bedivere and told him to draw his sword Excalibur from its sheath and carry it down to the margin of the lake.

'And when thou comest to the water side, I charge you throw my sword into the water, and then come again and tell me what you have seen,' he said, and sank back exhausted upon the ground.

Sir Bedivere took the sword and carried it down to the water's edge. But when he looked at the wonderful hilt of the weapon, all encrusted with gold and jewels and precious stones, a great temptation came to him.

'Why should I throw this marvellous sword into the water?' he said to himself. 'My lord the king is weak and ill, and knows not what he says. Were he well and in his right mind, to throw away his magic sword Excalibur would be the last thing he would require me to do. No good will come of it, if I do this wasteful deed.'

And instead of throwing the sword into the water, he hid it amongst the rushes at the side of the lake.

Then he went back to the ruined chapel, and as he reached it the king asked him eagerly:

'Did you throw the sword into the water?'

And Bedivere answered him untruly and said: 'Yes, oh king.'

'And what did you see?' asked Arthur.

'I saw nothing but the waves upon the lake,' said Bedivere.

The king's face grew dark with anger and disappointment.

'You have dealt unfaithfully with me,' he said. 'Had you done as I commanded you, some sign would have followed. Go quickly, and as you love me throw the sword into the water.'

Bedivere was ashamed of himself for having kept back the sword, and he ran quickly down to the lake and drew Excalibur from the place where he had hidden it and was about to throw it into the water, when again the rich sparkle of the jewels caught his eye. And once more temptation assailed him.

'It is a sin and shame to throw such a sword away,' he cried. And once more he hid it amongst the rushes and went back to the king, and told him untruthfully that he had done as he was told.

'And what did you hear or see?' asked Arthur faintly.

'Sir, I heard nothing but the water lapping on the shore, and I saw naught save the ripple washing in the reeds,' said Sir Bedivere.

'Ah, traitor!' cried Arthur in anger and distress. 'Twice have you dealt untruly with me. I little thought that you would have betrayed me for the handle of a sword! Once more will I send you. And this time if you do not as I command you, I will arise and slay you with mine own hands, dying though I be.'

Then Sir Bedivere was filled with remorse and penitence for his treachery to the dying king. He ran once more to the margin of the lake and took the sword up in his hands. And without giving himself time to think, he whirled the blade above his head and flung it far out over the waters of the lake.

And as the sword fell downward, a white arm rose out of the lake, and caught Excalibur by the hilt, waved it three times above the surface, and then vanished below the water again.

Sir Bedivere went back to the little chapel, and the king could see by the wonder in his eyes that this time he had done as he was commanded.

'Speak,' Arthur said. 'What have you seen?' And Bedivere told him what had happened when he had flung the sword into the lake.

Then Arthur gave a deep sigh of relief.

'Now help me to the water's edge,' he said.

'My end is nigh, it is time that I were gone. I fear me I have tarried overlong.'

Sir Bedivere took the king up in his arms and carried him down to the water's edge. As he reached the margin of the lake, a barge came gliding towards him, steered by women, all of whom were robed in black. Three queens wearing golden crowns upon their heads sat in the midst of the barge, and in the prow was standing a figure, whom Bedivere recognised with awe and wonder for the mysterious Lady of the Lake who had so often helped and protected Arthur in the past. When the barge came to land, the three queens held out their arms and took the dying king from Sir Bedivere and laid him in their laps. They wept and mourned as they received him, and one of the queens said :

'You have tarried overlong, my brother. This wound upon your head hath taken cold.'

Then the barge sailed slowly away from the land.

When Bedivere saw Arthur going away from him, a great feeling of desolation came upon him, and he stretched out his arms and cried out sorrowfully to the king.

'Alas, alas, my lord Arthur!' he cried. 'What shall become of me? Leave me not here alone in the midst of mine enemies.'

But the king answered him from the barge:

'Comfort yourself as best you may, for in me there is no help that you may trust in. I am going to the fair valley of Avalon to heal me of my grievous wound, and if you never hear more of me, pray for my soul.'

The barge moved away, while the black-robed women set up a dismal wailing and crying that filled Bedivere's heart with grief and fear. When the barge had quite disappeared from sight, the knight turned and went slowly away, weeping and mourning for the departure of the king and all the tragic things that had happened.

That was the end of the fellowship of the Round Table. Most of the knights who had formed the famous company were dead by this time, and those that were left either went into monasteries to pass the rest of their time on earth in prayer, or else went on Crusades and gave their lives fighting gloriously in foreign lands. Sir Lancelot, who had come to England with his followers to help the king against Mordred, grieved bitterly when he heard that he had come too late. He went at once to Guinevere and put himself and all his knights at her service, and would have carried her away to his own country and taken care of her all the rest of his life if she had wished him to. But Guinevere was broken-hearted by all that had passed, and she only wanted now to go into a nunnery, to take the 'way of perfection' as it was called in those days, and end her life in holiness and peace.

'Go you to your own realm and take a wife and live with her in joy and bliss,' she said to the knight. 'Only, for the love that has been between us, I beseech you pray for my soul.'

'You wish that I should return to my own country and wed a lady?' said Lancelot, smiling sadly. 'Nay, madam, that shall I never do. Since you are determined to take you unto perfection, then must I needs take me to perfection too. In you have I had all my earthly joy, and now for the little time that remaineth I also will give myself to God.'

Then these two, who had loved each other so dearly, said good-bye and parted. Lancelot went into a monastery and became a monk, while Guinevere became a nun and lived a life of prayer and devotion for a few years. Then she died, and Lancelot, who still loved her passionately, came and buried her.

The great knight did not live for long after the death of the queen whom he had loved so much.

Within a few weeks of her death he died too, and so these lovers were united at last. And perhaps they found death kinder to them than life had been.

This is the last of the stories of King Arthur and his knights. They are some of the most famous stories that have ever been told. Many books have been written about them, many wonderful poems and pictures and songs and noble deeds have they inspired, and will continue to inspire, so long as men love romance and beauty and the doing of great things. English-speaking men and women especially must be proud to think that all these wonderful stories of bravery and chivalry have been woven around the doings of an English king.

No man ever knew for certain what happened to Arthur when he was borne away from Bedivere's sight in the barge. Some say that Bedivere's delay in throwing the sword into the water cost the king his life, and that the black-robed women brought his body ashore and buried him in a little chapel not far from Glastonbury. But others say that they carried him away to the wonderful valley of Avalon, where it is always springtime and nothing can ever die, and all who go there grow young and strong again.

THE PASSING OF ARTHUR

And the legend runs that Arthur is living there still, waiting until England shall have need of him—when he will come with all his knights, Lancelot and Gawaine and Gareth and Galahad, and all who lived nobly and fought bravely in the wonderful days of old, to lead his people once more to victory and bring back the golden age of chivalry again.